The Integrated Guide to Treating Penetration Disorders in Women

Maha Nasrallah-Babenko presents a culturally sensitive and uniquely accessible guide that equips clinicians, student sex therapists, and female clients with the tools to confidently treat genito-pelvic pain and penetration disorders (GPPPD).

Addressing the issue from an integrated approach, the book provides evidence-based information and sensate, solo and partner practical exercises derived from the author's experience to help clinicians support women in redefining their relationship with sex, their bodies, and their partners. With a special focus on those from conservative and religious backgrounds, this beautifully illustrated text emphasizes the psychological, emotional, and relational factors that may increase shame and fear surrounding sex. The book defines GPPPD before outlining the author's ABCs approach, awareness, body, control, and safety, where she examines topics such as sexual abuse, how to communicate with your partner, sexual beliefs and messages, the importance of arousal, vulnerability and assertiveness, and shifting the significance of penetration for an enjoyable sex life.

This book is essential reading for training and established sex therapists, family therapists, and couple therapists looking to support those struggling with sexual intimacy, as well as the couples seeking their help.

Maha Nasrallah-Babenko is a licensed Psychologist with a PhD in Psychology and a Diploma in Psychosexual and Relationship Therapy. She is from Lebanon and is currently based in the US.

"Psychosexual Therapy might be difficult to define, a difficult marriage of medicine, psychology, and human systems. Dr. Nasrallah-Babenko confidently navigates this relationship and adds to it up-to-date research on the subject of penetration disorders. She examines, critically, the transgenerational and cultural injunctions which influence women (and those clinicians who work with them) in their sexual development. She explores those methodologies aimed at repairing and overcoming women's psychosexual issues and ultimately assists couples in growing together. This work is pioneering in that it focuses on women in the Middle East; it comes highly recommended as a resource for clinicians and trainers in the field and particularly those who might wish to critique the field from a transcultural perspective."

Bernd Leygraf, *Consultant Psychotherapist,*
Naos-Institute (www.naos-institute.com)

"I recommend this book to students, clinicians, and clients. Maha Nasrallah-Babenko has captured the essence of working with a dedicated client group who frequently present with issues concerned with pain, non-consummation, and sexual naivety. The content is easily readable and demonstrates empathy for the clients, walking with them to a potentially positive outcome. Whilst the client group is specific, there is no doubt that the recommendations, exercises, and insights would be useful to a broader population of women who attend for psychosexual and relationship therapy. There is a balance of work contained within the book, which is stabilizing and holding for the clients and, as such, should be added to dedicated course reading lists for students in the field. This book will be used frequently and become one of the 'go to' texts for some time to come."

Judi Keshet-Orr, *Founder/Director LDPRT*
(www.psychosexualtraining.org.uk)

The Integrated Guide to Treating Penetration Disorders in Women

Transforming Sexual Relationships from Fear to Confidence

Maha Nasrallah-Babenko, PhD

NEW YORK AND LONDON

First published 2022
by Routledge
605 Third Avenue, New York, NY 10158

and by Routledge
2 Park Square, Milton Park, Abingdon, Oxon OX14 4RN

Routledge is an imprint of the Taylor & Francis Group, an informa business

© 2022 Maha Nasrallah-Babenko

The right of Maha Nasrallah-Babenko to be identified as author of this work has been asserted by her in accordance with sections 77 and 78 of the Copyright, Designs and Patents Act 1988.

Illustrations by Kendra Profumo, BFA, MS

All rights reserved. No part of this book may be reprinted or reproduced or utilised in any form or by any electronic, mechanical, or other means, now known or hereafter invented, including photocopying and recording, or in any information storage or retrieval system, without permission in writing from the publishers.

Trademark notice: Product or corporate names may be trademarks or registered trademarks, and are used only for identification and explanation without intent to infringe.

Library of Congress Cataloging-in-Publication Data
A catalog record for this title has been requested

ISBN: 978-0-367-65376-7 (hbk)
ISBN: 978-0-367-65377-4 (pbk)
ISBN: 978-1-00-312917-2 (ebk)

DOI: 10.4324/9781003129172

Typeset in Bembo
by Newgen Publishing UK

This book is dedicated to every woman who has been told or made to feel, one way or another, that she (or her body) was broken, that she was not good enough, or that she was too much.

I want to also dedicate this to my mom and dad, who will always be the people I want to make most proud.

Lastly, I would like to dedicate this book to my friend Kim, whose life was taken away from us way too soon because of COVID-19, but whose supportive and loving voice will always be with us.

Contents

Foreword ix
Preface xiii
Acknowledgments xv
Introduction xvii

1 General Overview of Genito-Pelvic Pain/Penetration Disorders   1
 What Is Vaginismus/GPPPD? 1
 How Vaginismus Develops 4
 Presentation of Penetration Disorders 8
 Therapeutic Interventions for Clinician and Client 17

2 Psychological and Emotional Factors   21
 Expectations Around Sex 22
 Myths and Unhealthy Beliefs About Sex 24
 Shame and Disgust 33
 Trauma and Sexual Abuse 39

3 Between Control and Vulnerability   41
 The Purpose of Vaginismus 41
 Assertiveness 43
 Authenticity 48
 Letting Go 50

4 Relational Factors   54
 The Effect on and Role of the Partner 55
 The Relationship Foundation 60
 Communication Skills 64

5 Mastering Her Body   69
 Pelvic Floor Strengthening 69
 Mindfulness, Relaxation, and Grounding 71

Self-Sensate 74
Solo Genital Exposure Progressions 89

6 Incorporating the Partner   96
Sensate Focus Overview and Purpose 97
Sensate Focus Program 100
Partner-Assisted Genital Exposure 107
Completing the Process 111

Conclusion: Closing Words and Beyond   116

Index   123

Foreword

Dr. Maha Nasrallah-Babenko, the author of this book, is a woman full of energy and determination as well as a sharp creative intelligence and much warmth. I have known her for over a decade and enjoyed and admired her dynamic presence navigating the field of psychosexual therapy. In the time I have known her, she has moved from London to Beirut to the UAE and now the US! Her interests have included rock climbing and equine therapy which I feel gives some indication of her adventurous personality and willingness to grapple with challenge.

That she has now written a book that I feel will be tremendously helpful to the profession is not a surprise, as she would speak of her desire to be in a position to do so from the early days of her training. She realized the real need for more dissemination of information for psychosexual practitioners. I still eagerly await the book on rapid ejaculation she would speak of writing then, as her early clients, while she was training, nearly all seemed to come to her with that presenting issue. I first met her when she was embarking on the London Diploma in Psychosexual and Relationship Therapy (LDPRT) whilst working on her PhD in Psychology at University College London; doing both of these simultaneously is itself quite an undertaking, let alone the fact that her home base was in Beirut whilst the training was in London. I was a tutor and supervisor on the LDPRT at that time, and am now one of the course directors and, along with my estimable fellow course directors, Judi Keshet-Orr and Bernd Leygraf, am happy to have remained in close contact with Maha.

This book arises from Maha's years of working in the UAE when she became aware of the prevalence of women clients coming to her office to seek help for the painful and stressful experiences they were having sexually. She saw the need for books for practitioners, both therapeutic and medical, in helping women specifically within the religious, traditional culture of the Middle East, with a sensitive understanding of their needs and the context within which they presented. Her understanding of that very specific client group shines through her book. They are mainly married women in religious communities, many from arranged marriages with no previous sexual experience. They would come to her office because they had been married, sometimes for years, and had not been able to "consummate the marriage" – wanting to feel free of fear and shame and, often, motivated by wanting to have children. The book reflects how her work as a psychosexual therapist embraces that remit, along with bringing her own unique, integrative, and ethical stance.

The book can be seen as a useful guide to working with all forms of genito-pelvic pain and penetration disorders (GPPPD), with a particular focus on vaginismus. In terms of her psychosexual understanding, she has incorporated understanding gained in this area from writers, therapists, and scientists such as Rosemary Basson, Ellen Laan, and Emily Nagoski. Apart from wanting to help alleviate pain, fear, shame, and distress, Maha writes of wanting women to feel relaxed about sex and their bodies, confident about themselves, and having trust and understanding in their relationships and even to feel desire and enjoy sex!

Although the book has the specific readership of therapists and medics working with the client group described in mind, there is much here of benefit to practitioners everywhere. As a trainer of psychosexual and relationship therapists, I would encourage our students to learn from Maha's wisdom and experience. The Western sociocultural context may be very different from that of the clients Maha is discussing in her book but, otherwise, the approach is to the individual woman, as it would be, anywhere else. The sociocultural context is, of course, highly significant, and that is a possibly unique feature of this book. It is a brave and remarkable endeavor, to write such a detailed, universally applicable, guide to working with such a sensitive and important psychosexual difficulty, whilst targeting this large but underacknowledged client group. Vaginismus sufferers everywhere need the understanding of the condition and how to treat it that this book conveys in careful and compassionate detail. Given this client group, there is little detail on working with gender, sexual, and relationship diversity but this understanding, necessary to a therapist or medic working with a less conservative client group, can, indeed should, be integrated by the therapist, as Maha acknowledges. It is important to recognize that women everywhere often suffer shame and anxiety with this difficulty, as do people with any psychosexual difficulty.

This book explains clearly how to work with these feelings, as well as giving full instructions on using the nuts and bolts of the traditional practical exercises and much else besides. Maha also, for example, writes in detail, helpfully, about how to reach and dispel the myths a client may have heard that have exacerbated a fearful attitude toward sex.

Rather than expecting therapists to leap into setting the physical exercises, therapists are encouraged to be alert to the possibility of trauma in the client and to be prepared to refer them to individual therapy and, if there are serious relationship issues, to couples therapy. It also encourages awareness of the possibility of domestic abuse or of current or historic sexual abuse.

Maha's approach is highly integrative. She makes it clear that women with vaginismus require a "multidimensional approach." This is in keeping with the training she undertook with the LDPRT which espouses a biopsychosocial approach, integrating an understanding of the medical and physical aspects with the sociocultural context, the relational factors, and the psychological. All of this understanding is engaged with an emphasis on a psychotherapeutic client/therapist relationship. Whilst she is highly rational and uses CBT, a humanistic, psychotherapeutic approach is also described as her preferred way of working with a client. Maha will ask philosophical questions of her clients by, for example, asking them to consider their values. She may also ask what the function of vaginismus is for them:

> The body shares a lot of wisdom, and we just need to learn to listen better. Understanding what the client's body is trying to do for her can help us support her through creating the mental, physical, and emotional environment that she needs in order to feel safe and confident.

Throughout this book, there is much wisdom to be found. An emphasis is evident on the need for therapy to help build qualities in the client to help them in their psychosexual growth, such as assertiveness and authenticity. There is also wisdom in the support for couples, expressed beautifully in passages such as:

> It is about empowering both partners to hold on to their own selves and be connected at the same time. Meaningful connection is not a constant experience, it happens in moments; couples ebb and flow between separateness and connection. As Gibran Khalil Gibran said, "Let there be spaces in your togetherness."

Jean Miller, a Course Director of the London Diploma in Psychosexual Therapy and a Psychosexual and Relationship Psychotherapist. UKCP Reg, COSRT seniorAccred.
15 December 2020

Preface

Growing up, I never dreamed that I would end up becoming a sex therapist. In fact, I highly doubt that any young child would think of that as their future career! I do remember always being interested in the medical and helping fields though. I went from wanting to be a surgeon, to wanting to be a veterinarian, to then realizing that I was actually deeply passionate about psychology and understanding the human mind. While I was completing my PhD in Psychology at University College London, I had a lightbulb moment during a conversation I was having with my sisters about relationships. I realized that I wanted to be a sex and relationship therapist! As soon as I started my Diploma in Psychosexual and Relationship Therapy training in London (www.psychosexualtraining.org.uk), I knew I was right where I wanted to be.

I have been asked several times throughout my career what drew me to this field. Through some conversations and self-reflection I realized that one of the reasons, among many others, was that it was my way of pushing the boundaries and creating positive change in our society – my own revolution. I grew up in quite a confusing culture; on the one hand, the Lebanese people are very open-minded, liberal, and Westernized, and on the other, we are still conservative and traditional in some ways. And so many of us (especially women) receive mixed messages about sex and relationships throughout our life. In a society that is so modern and outgoing, where young people date and party, we still hold a lot of shame and guilt around sexuality, and thus only express certain desires of ours in secret. I was never the overtly rebellious type, and so I've always tried to integrate the parts of myself that wanted to conform and be accepted with the other parts that wanted to be free and authentic, in an appropriate and positive manner. Consequently, I think that one of the ways I was able to do that was by working through my own feelings about sex and relationships and providing others with the space and opportunity for them to do the same.

As a result, my career and life choices took me from London, to Beirut, to Dubai, to New York City, to Southern California, and to Colorado, where I currently live with my husband, Bo, and our dog, Lexi – and who knows where our adventures will take us in the future! Having lived and practiced in different countries, I am eternally grateful and lucky to have worked with people from various cultures, backgrounds, religions, and sexual orientations. I feel that growing up in Lebanon and having been exposed to both the conservative and liberal cultures myself have also given me an edge in being able to understand some of my clients better. I continue to enjoy and love my work every day and am deeply grateful to all of the clients who have trusted me with their most vulnerable moments. Writing a book is one of the ways I wanted to give back to society and make a positive impact on a larger scale.

I started writing this book sometime in 2018. I had some thoughts I wanted to share and would write a chapter or two, and then stop for a few weeks or months at a time. I did not feel ready or courageous enough at the time to put my work out there just yet. In 2019, I kept thinking about it and started exploring the possibilities of whether I wanted to self-publish or work with a publisher. Then 2020 came around, and COVID-19 happened, and somehow I was motivated again to pursue the book and so I reached out to a few publishers. I got confirmation once again from the universe that things happen at the time they are meant to happen when Heather, my editor, took an interest in my book, and living in the time of COVID-19 gave me the time I needed to complete it. When other people were coping with the lockdowns by taking up a new hobby like baking or knitting, or having babies, I birthed a book.

Acknowledgments

Where do I begin? Creating this would have never been possible without the support and presence of countless people in my life.

I would firstly like to thank all of my clients; it is because of their courage to share their stories and journeys with me that I can continue to learn and share how to better help others.

My deepest gratitude goes to my husband, Bo, for always believing in me and being the person who continuously shows me what it means to be loved for who you are.

Thank you to our dog Lexi who kept me company in the office for many hours as I worked on this, and distracted me at the perfect times when she knew I needed a break or a walk.

I, of course, would not be here without the endless of my whole family; especially my parents, my siblings, and Fhe. I am eternally grateful for the sacrifices my parents made to give me every opportunity they could to pursue my ambitions and dreams.

I am also very touched by the wholehearted encouragement and loving presence of so many of my wonderful friends, such as Leila, Chris, Raina, Maria, Mona, Dina, Najib, Carine, Heather, and Maya. The year I was finishing the manuscript was especially meaningful to me as a Lebanese woman living far away from my family and friends in Lebanon, as 2020 was an extremely painful year for the Lebanese people. Not only did they endure the universal trauma of a pandemic, they were also faced with a severe economic crisis, and suffered a horrifically large explosion that led to around 200 deaths and thousands of injured victims.

A very heartfelt thank-you also goes out to Jean Miller, my supervisor and friend, who helped me believe in myself as an author and continues to nurture my growth as a therapist.

So much gratitude goes to Judi Keshet-Orr and Bernd Leygraf, for their continuous support and wisdom, and everyone else from my Diploma who gave me the foundation I have today.

A huge thank-you also goes to Kendra Profumo, who generously created and offered the beautiful illustrations for this book, and whose work continues to inspire me and other women.

I feel very blessed to have been able to connect with Dr. Jessica O'Reilly and other people I look up to in the field. And I am immensely grateful for Keri Nola and all of the healers I connected with through her for providing a community and holding a safe space as I worked through all of the stages of the process.

My colleagues and friends like Jessica Mathon, Jennifer Schilling, Dr. Tufia Steidle, Dr. Deema Sihweil, and Dr. Thoraiya Kanafani are also people I will always hold very warmly in my heart.

And of course, a big thanks goes to Heather Evans, my editor, for not only publishing this book, but also making the process easier and more enjoyable than I could ever have imagined, and to Upasruti and the team at Routledge for helping make this a reality.

The list can go on and on. Every person who touched my life in one way or another, from Lebanon, to London, Dubai, and the USA, even if you were not named here, helped in my evolution as a person and therapist, and in the birth of this work.

It is thanks to all of these people that some women and couples around the world are going to have another resource to help them heal.

Introduction

The dread of the wedding night still haunts many women. Throughout my years of practice in the United Arab Emirates (UAE), vaginismus and unconsummated marriages due to vaginismus or vaginal penetration phobia were the most common difficulties women and couples from Middle-Eastern, Arab, and South-Asian cultures presented to me. That was very different from my prior experience practicing in Lebanon, and so far in the United States, where I was sought out by far fewer clients for these particular issues. I also noticed that most of the clients I worked with in the UAE, along with the majority of the population out there including some health professionals, did not have access to accurate and sufficient sexual education, if any. They also did not have appropriate or accessible resources, such as books, social support, and medical professionals, to seek information or help from when they did experience difficulties.

Although many useful books and resources are available online or around the world, I found that they did not discuss or address some pertinent cultural considerations specific to this region, nor did they tackle the issue from a complete perspective, and they were not available in their native languages. Taking all of these points into consideration, I decided to write a holistic book based on my clinical approach that would address the issue from different angles, and include culturally sensitive and relevant information based on my clinical experience in the region. This book, therefore, is meant to be mostly an expression of my professional approach, knowledge, and experience.

My main motivation behind writing this book was to provide a resource for therapists and medical professionals who work with or encounter such issues in their practice, in order to share with them some of the unique cultural, relational, and individual factors that I found were helpful in guiding my work with clients. Additionally, I wanted this resource to be accessible to women and couples in the Middle East, South Asia, and the rest of the world who are experiencing vaginismus or similar issues and do not have access to specialized professional help. Therefore, though this book is specifically aimed at clinicians who work with Middle-Eastern, Arab, and South-Asian women and couples from religious backgrounds who are struggling to consummate their marriage, any woman or couple who desires penetrative sex and is having difficulties with it, whatever their marital status, sexual history, or religious/cultural background, may also benefit.

The information provided in this book is not meant to replace the training or approach that clinicians working with clients suffering from penetration difficulties use. Instead, I encourage them to rely on their judgment and intuition and take from it what they find useful to them, and modify any exercises or suggestions according to the needs of their clients. As for the women or couples from the general public who are searching for information and guidance on how to overcome their sexual challenges, they may find the information and method presented here to be a helpful resource. I would like to note, however, that I rarely follow the approach described in this book in a rigid and exact manner, as the process is usually fluid and each client has different needs. Therefore, I would also encourage the readers to use their intuition and seek out additional professional resources where available to support them through their difficulties in the best way possible. Regardless of who is reading this, my recommendation would be to read the whole book even if they reach a section that either was sufficient for them to resolve their issues or did not resonate with them, so that they can make the most of this process and take in whatever feels most supportive to them.

Almost all of my female clients who were having difficulty with vaginal penetrative sex were either married or in a committed relationship. My general recommendation for my clients while attempting to resolve the issue (whether it is with the guidance of this book, or in therapy, or on their own), is to stop any sexual activity that causes stress and/or pain, or reinforces negative feelings around sex (especially attempting vaginal penetrative sex) until she reaches the specific stage (later in this book) that encourages the practice or attempt of that particular sexual activity. If it is only vaginal penetrative sex that causes stress, then they may engage in other sexual activities together that feel safe and good to her. It is important that she communicates with her partner about what feels comfortable for her and what she is not ready to do at this stage, and for them to come to an agreement on the boundaries while working through her fears. For example, if they agree not to have any vaginal intercourse throughout this process, they can negotiate other activities that provide intimacy and sexual pleasure for both that are within her comfort level, such as giving or receiving manual stimulation or oral sex. Some of this is based on the work of Masters and Johnson, but this approach has been honed, modernized, and refined to fit the target population of this book.

If the client is not in a relationship while seeking professional help, she can still benefit from the information or guidance of this book and reach a more confident and relaxed state regarding her genitals and sex. There are also several exercises that she can work through individually that will help her overcome some of her difficulties, and these may be sufficient for her to overcome her discomfort or fears. However, there are partner exercises she will probably not be able to benefit from until she is in a safe and trusting relationship with someone who is willing to collaborate with and support her through the process.

Important information: If at any point of this treatment guide anything feels too difficult and/or intense, or is bringing up some deeper unresolved emotional or psychological issue or trauma, I would recommend that the client stops this treatment and seeks professional help from a trained and qualified mental health practitioner to address these specific events. If the client or her partner suffers from any other psychological or mental disorder, then I suggest that they seek appropriate treatment from a mental health professional before starting this treatment. If the client and her partner are in crisis or experiencing severe relationship distress, I strongly recommend that they attend couples therapy with a trained professional before starting this treatment.

Please note that, though this book aims to help practitioners in their work with clients who want to overcome their penetration difficulties and sexual fears, it is not meant to help other significant relationship issues. If the client and her partner have a respectful and loving relationship, this book is written to help them complete their intimate and sexual life, but it will not help with other deep or serious relationship problems. If the client has any unresolved history of sexual abuse or trauma, I strongly advise that she does not follow this treatment alone, and that she seeks the guidance of a trauma-informed qualified mental health professional.

Additionally, the majority of cases I worked with suffering from penetration difficulties were clients who identified as cis-gender women (women whose gender identity matches the biological sex they were assigned at birth) in heterosexual relationships. And so while, for that reason, the book is written using heteronormative language (heteronormative meaning everyone is presumed straight), it is not meant to dismiss readers or clients who identify with a different gender or sexual orientation. These types of disorders can occur in women regardless of their sexual orientation, and so though the partner exercises described are based on heterosexual couples, they can be modified to work for non-heterosexual couples as well. For example, instead of using a penis, the partner can participate by using her fingers and other appropriate objects/sex toys.

Furthermore, in order to maintain the privacy and confidentiality of my clients, the case examples provided throughout this book are not based on one specific client per se. Instead, they are general descriptions of common stories, traits, and experiences I came across with clients. Therefore, the names, ages, and other identifying information are made up, and the characters are a blend of several clients that I worked with who shared similar experiences.

The first chapter of the book will go over the description of genito-pelvic pain and penetration disorders (GPPPD), with a focus on what is known as "vaginismus." I explain its symptoms, development, and presentation, specifically in women from conservative cultures, in addition to the main contributing factors involved. A brief description of the overall framework behind therapeutic interventions of GPPPD will also be provided as an introduction to my approach.

Chapter 2 discusses the importance of offering information and raising awareness around sex, the genitals, and arousal when working with clients. Unrealistic expectations and beliefs that contribute to negative associations around sex are challenged and modified, as are some of the commonly held myths around sex. How shame and disgust develop, and the impact of sexual trauma and abuse, are explored in greater depth to support the client in processing and resolving these feelings and experiences.

The third chapter focuses on helping the client strengthen some of the psychological and intra-personal skills that contribute to the woman feeling more confident in life. The goal is for her to regain a sense of control by practicing assertiveness and setting boundaries, while also learning to let go of dysfunctional anxiety. Suggestions and discussions around how to live and connect more authentically, how to be more relaxed, and how to feel more empowered are provided to the clinician to help them support the women through this personal development journey.

Chapter 4 discusses the relational aspect of my approach in working with women. The effect of the vaginismus on the partner is discussed, in addition to how the partner may be unintentionally contributing to or maintaining the difficulties. Safety (emotional and physical) is crucial for women to be able to let go and figuratively and literally let their partners in; therefore, it is important for the couple to work on strengthening their emotional connection and building trust. Information and suggestions around how to express and feel love and how to communicate and listen effectively are provided in order to support the client and her partner through creating a healthy relationship foundation.

Chapter 5 describes the individual behavioral and practical exercises of the treatment that help women gain more control over their pelvic muscles, explore their body and sensuality, and practice vaginal dilation by mindfully and gradually exposing their genital area to progressive degrees of vaginal penetration.

Once the woman successfully completes the individual exercises and feels more prepared for incorporating her partner, the treatment then focuses on the Sensate Focus program for the couple to engage in, followed by partner-assisted genital exposure exercises, which are described in the sixth chapter. The aim here is to help the client build arousal and comfort with her partner, and support the couple through progressively achieving different stages of penetration until they attempt and complete vaginal penetrative sex.

Lastly, the book concludes with a brief summary and suggestions for clients who wish to explore their sexuality beyond consummation.

It is important to note that the order of the chapters does not necessarily reflect the order of the type of work I am focusing on with the client. Usually, I start early on in the process with some of the individual exercises described in Chapter 5 while discussing, alongside the behavioral work, some of the psychological, emotional, and relational factors presented in Chapters

2, 3, and 4. I chose to write the chapters in the order presented to encourage the reader to incorporate the mental, emotional, and inter-personal in the process, as opposed to just focusing on the exercises. Lastly, though this book mainly targets clinicians, the language in the sections that describes a specific exercise is written addressing the client directly, in order to simplify it and make it easier to use as an exercise in and of itself.

1 General Overview of Genito-Pelvic Pain/Penetration Disorders

What Is Vaginismus/GPPPD?

According to the DSM-IV (American Psychiatric Association, 2000), which is the diagnostic manual that psychologists and other mental health professionals follow in their assessment and diagnosis of psychological disorders, vaginismus is defined as:

> Recurrent or persistent involuntary spasm of the musculature of the outer third of the vagina that interferes with coitus and causes marked distress or interpersonal difficulty. The condition cannot be better accounted for by another Axis I disorder and is not caused exclusively by a physical disorder.

In other words, vaginismus is a condition where the woman consistently experiences involuntary contractions of her vaginal muscles which causes difficulties with penetration and leads to significant personal or relationship distress.

Often vaginismus makes penis-in-vagina (PIV) sex impossible and can be the cause of an unconsummated marriage. Although the muscular spasms that occur in vaginismus can help the condition be diagnosed (by a qualified gynecologist, pelvic physical therapist, or family doctor), diagnostic agreement between different clinicians has been shown to be poor; vaginal pain and spasms did not differentiate between women with vaginismus and dyspareunia (a genital pain disorder; i.e. painful sex) resulting from vulvar vestibulitis (Reissing et al., 2004) In addition, many of the health professionals usually involved in the assessment of vaginismus have insufficient expertise in diagnosing the muscular spasm, not to mention there being a lack of consensus around which muscles are involved in the spasms. Furthermore, it is difficult to discern whether the vaginal spasms have developed as a defense to painful attempts, or whether the spasms are what cause the pain. Some women with vaginismus display similar characteristics as people with specific phobias (hence why I sometimes use the term vaginal penetration phobia) (Lahaie et al., 2010). Fear of pain is the primary reason for some women with vaginismus abstaining from and avoiding sex, and so the previous classification of vaginismus does not take enough into account how fear plays into its development.

These are some of the reasons why the new version of the DSM (fifth edition) combined vaginismus, dyspareunia, and other penetration disorders into one main and broader diagnosis: genito-pelvic pain/penetration disorders (GPPPD) (American Psychiatric Association, 2013). The new DSM-V guidelines specify that if the woman has recurrent and distressing difficulty with one (or more) of the following for at least six months, then a GPPPD diagnosis is warranted:

- vaginal penetration during intercourse
- marked vulvovaginal or pelvic pain during intercourse or attempted intercourse
- marked fear or anxiety about the experience of vaginal or pelvic pain as related to vaginal penetration
- marked tensing of the pelvic floor muscles during attempted vaginal penetration

(Perez & Binik, 2016)

I should note that, though the diagnoses of vaginismus, dyspareunia, and other penetration difficulties have been merged into GPPPD, the treatment guideline I describe in this book is mostly based on my work with women who suffered from either vaginismus or vaginal penetration phobia (which, together, I will refer to as "penetration disorders" throughout the book), and not dyspareunia. And so though many of the suggestions in this book could also be beneficial in treating painful sex, it must be noted that they may not be appropriate or sufficient for some of these cases. I may use the terms GPPPD, vaginismus, or penetration disorders interchangeably throughout the book to refer to the condition. If PIV sex or attempted vaginal penetrative sex is painful, it may be useful for the client to consult a pelvic physical therapist (if they are available where the client resides) for a complete evaluation to assess whether there may be organic or physical causes for the pain. If the client has no access to a physical therapist specializing in pelvic issues, then they may consult a qualified gynecologist instead.

Prior to the development of the GPPPD diagnosis in the DSM-V, I personally did not rely solely on identifying muscular spasms for the diagnosis of vaginismus. Whenever a client presented to me with a self-report of either not being able to have PIV sex, complete a gynecological exam, or insert a tampon, I would treat the condition in a similar manner. My preferred definition has thus been inspired by Basson et al. (2004) who recommend the following guidelines:

> The persistent or recurrent difficulties of a woman to allow vaginal entry of a penis, a finger, and or any object, despite a woman's expressed wish to do so. There is often (phobic) avoidance and anticipation/fear/

experience of pain, along with variable involuntary pelvic muscle contraction. Structural or other physical abnormalities must be ruled out/addressed.

So to put it simply, if a woman is unable to have vaginal penetrative sex or insert a tampon or have a gynecological exam due to either fear or uncontrollable muscle contractions, despite her desire to do so, and this difficulty is causing her distress, then I would approach it similarly to treating vaginismus, with a great focus on her fears and discomfort. Even if she is not experiencing muscle contractions and is merely experiencing an uncontrollable phobic response or avoidance (specific phobia linked to sex or vaginal penetration), I would follow the same guidelines. In other words, one way in which GPPPD may show up is that the couple may be attempting vaginal penetrative sex and the penis might not be able to enter the vagina because there is a tightening/tensing of her vaginal and pelvic muscles, or because of pain. Alternatively, the couple may not actually be having any penile-vaginal contact and they are unable to have PIV sex because of the woman's avoidance behaviors such as tightening and closing of the legs, pushing the partner away, or moving away from the partner. In both situations there is an experience or anticipation of pain and/or vaginal penetration, and in my opinion, it is that experience or fear that is underlying vaginismus or dyspareunia in many women (Leiblum, 2007, p. 125). Though the treatment plans in both cases generally look the same in my approach, they will and should, of course, be tailored to each individual according to her needs, circumstances, and severity. Therefore, this book offers a general guide to overcoming this difficulty, which I encourage the reader to modify according to what they deem would be best for their client or situation.

Vaginismus may arise as part of a conditioning response that is acquired secondarily to negative physical and/or psychological stimuli. This means that a woman can associate sex or any other penetrative activity with physical pain, fear, or trauma, if she experienced one (or more) incident(s) where the physical or psychological stimuli were present at the same time as a sexual or genital experience. It is one of the most common female sexual dysfunctions – prevalence rate is not accurately known and varies in different parts of the world (figures range from 5 percent to 43 percent depending on where the data was collected and how it has been classified, and tends to be higher in Muslim-populated countries) (Oksuz & Malhan, 2006; Perez, Brown, & Binik, 2016; Nobre, Pinto-Gouveia, & Gomez, 2006; Laumann, Paik, & Rosen, 1999; Lau, Kim, & Tsui, 2005; Leiblum, 2007, p. 130). I can confidently say that it was the most common presenting issue Arab and South-Asian women would bring to me in therapy during my years practicing in the UAE, which supports some of the evidence that it tends to be more common in more conservative and religious parts of the world.

What Is Dyspareunia?

Though this book is not about dyspareunia specifically, I am going to briefly describe it, as some women suffer from it in addition to vaginismus and separating the two can get confusing. As vaginismus and dyspareunia can be a common comorbidity (co-occurring diagnoses), it is likely that this is one of the reasons they have been merged into one main category. Put simply, dyspareunia is recurrent genital pain associated with sexual activity (could be superficial/external, vaginal, or deep). It is usually used to describe pain on penetration but can occur during genital stimulation. In situations where dyspareunia is an issue, I highly recommend stopping any activity that is painful, and consulting a gynecologist or pelvic physical therapist to check for any potential physical abnormality, or medical/organic cause such as infection, inflammation, endometriosis, or cysts.

If no medical cause is found, it is often a result of insufficient lubrication and/or low arousal, which generally happens if the woman is not relaxed (such as if she has vaginismus or is anxious/fearful), and/or is not excited enough (for example, if she has low desire, or is not attracted to the partner, or is anxious, or not stimulated in the appropriate manner). At times paying more attention to sensual touch and appropriate sexual stimulation helps, if it is mainly a matter of creating more arousal. And sometimes couples therapy may be advised if problems in the relationship are leading to a lack of interest in or aversion to sex. Though this book discusses the integrated treatment of penetration disorders, which are part of GPPPD, I cannot claim that it can also treat painful sex, as there could be other potential factors involved in pain. What I can say, however, is that incorporating some of the themes or exercises provided in this book could potentially be helpful in addressing the pain, depending on the specific case and causes.

How Vaginismus Develops

Like many other psychological or medical issues, it can be very difficult to find a cause for vaginismus. Generally speaking, however, a combination of contributing factors can be associated with vaginismus. Some of these factors, such as traumatic events, can act as triggering factors, while other predisposing factors, such as one's upbringing, make the woman susceptible to potentially developing a sexual dysfunction. There are also maintaining factors, such as some of the partner's behaviors or relationship dynamics that may be either exacerbating or maintaining the issue.

Contributing Factors

- Fear of pain or fear of tearing during penetration (Fadul et al., 2019): may be due to stories they have heard about sex being painful, scary, traumatic, or involving a lot of blood.

General Overview of GPPPD 5

- Fear of losing control over the body or situation (Fadul et al., 2019), fear of the unknown: not being able to predict or know what sex is going to feel like, how they may react or behave during (for example, if they are going to have a panic attack or do things that may be embarrassing), and whether or not they will enjoy it. This fear may also involve the fear of not knowing how their partner is going to act during sex (for example, if they are going to be rough or lose control).
- Childhood sexual trauma: molestation, sexual assault, and sexual abuse experienced during childhood. Sexual abuse is discussed further in Chapter 2.
- Sexual assault: sexual harassment, sexual assault, or rape during adulthood.
- Religious/conservative background: recent studies from Turkey and other predominantly Muslim countries suggest a very high prevalence of vaginismus. These reports are consistent with older clinical reports from other highly religious groups (Perez & Binik, 2016).
- Familial, religious, and cultural taboos, shame and guilt associated with sex, and high emphasis on virginity: this is related to the previous point but also different in that it is specifically about being exposed to negative messages and information around sex in one's environment due to cultural, religious, or familial taboos.
- Authoritarian/abusive parenting style: more women with vaginismus reported being educated under authoritarian/abusive environments than controls (Fadul et al., 2019).
- Lack of sexual education: many countries and cultures lack any sex education at school or in the household, which can lead to inaccurate and unrealistic beliefs about sex.
- Inadequate sexual information: even when sex education is provided in some schools and countries, it often covers the main biological and anatomical information about sex, thus lacking useful insights around some of the important psychological, social, and relational aspects involved in sex. When education or information about sex is inadequate, that could also contribute to the development of unrealistic and harmful beliefs and behaviors around sex.
- Unrealistic sexual beliefs/fantasies (e.g. the vagina is too small to accommodate a penis): when sex education is inadequate or lacking, or children and adults gather incorrect information about sex from peers or unreliable sources, one can then develop unrealistic expectations about sex, which could lead to shame, anxiety, fear, and guilt around sex.
- Painful or traumatic first attempt: when a woman experiences a painful or traumatic first attempt, this could condition her to associate pain or fear with sex. As a result, she could then anticipate pain in future attempts, and ultimately experience fear and/or pain during sex. This will be discussed further throughout the book.
- Physical pain caused by some medical issues such as genital tract infections, vestibulitis, postmenopausal estrogen deficiency, trauma

associated with genital surgery and radiotherapy, problems with arousal that result in poor lubrication and consequently painful vaginal penetrative sex (arousal dysfunction is more common in women with diabetes, multiple sclerosis, or spinal cord injury).
- Traumatic gynecological examinations by unsympathetic health professionals: similar to the painful or traumatic first attempt, if the woman experiences a painful or traumatic medical exam, she could then associate pain with objects penetrating or even approaching her genital area.
- Relationship problems (may lead to or maintain vaginismus or other sexual difficulties): relationship factors could contribute to the development or maintenance of penetration difficulties by creating a lack of emotional (or even physical) safety in the relationship.
- Fear of pregnancy: though this fear is often subconscious or minimized, it could contribute to the woman finding penetrative sex difficult. At times even if sex is protected and safe, fears around pregnancy can sometimes be irrational due to underlying anxiety and guilt around sex.
- Anxious personality traits: having anxiety or finding it difficult to have a flexible and relaxed mindset could contribute to the woman needing to control situations that are unknown or that she is not fully in control of. Sex could be one of those situations. This is again elaborated further later in the book. Women with vaginismus tend to experience higher levels of pain catastrophizing cognitions and harm avoidance (Borg et al., 2012).
- Being with an inexperienced partner: this is mostly related to the woman feeling confident and safe during sex. Having an inexperienced partner who does not exhibit confidence during sex could contribute to the woman feeling less safe and more anxious, especially when attempting something that is new to her that she does not feel confident in either.
- Failure to communicate: the inability of the couple to openly communicate about sex specifically can perpetuate the sexual negative cycle or exacerbate the issue.

There is suggestion of a cycle that evolves where fear and anticipation of pain, leading to some muscular tension/contraction, increases the likelihood of future penetration attempts resulting in a sensation of pain – this then leads to avoidance of future penetration attempts, thus reinforcing the avoidance due to relief of the fear (as shown in Figure 1.1). As briefly described above, the fear and anticipation of pain could develop from several of the contributing factors, such as painful/traumatic first attempts, experiences, or gynecological exams, insufficient or inadequate sexual information, unrealistic beliefs about sex, and anxiety or lack of safety.

Case Example

Zaynab, who is from the UAE, shares the story of many young women from the Arab and South-Asian worlds. She got married in her early twenties to a young man she met through her family who is part of her community, grew up in a

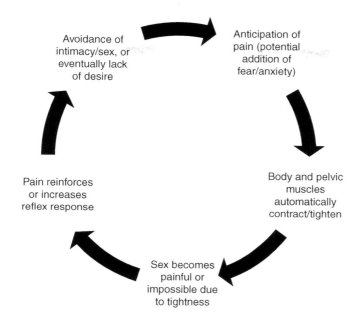

Figure 1.1 Vaginismus pain cycle.

religious family, did not receive much sex education, and heard some women in her extended family and circle of friends talk about traumatic first sexual experiences that were very painful and bloody. On their wedding night, they were both tired but still attempted vaginal penetrative sex as it was the "normal" and expected thing to do. She could not forget the scary stories she had heard about sex and was very nervous during. They did not engage in much touch or other forms of sexual intimacy and went straight to attempting vaginal intercourse. Her legs were tense and contracted but she tried really hard to keep them open and allow him to penetrate her. She was also not very lubricated due to her anxiety and lack of erotic build-up which did not help create sufficient arousal. As soon as the tip of his penis pushed into the entry of her vagina she felt a sharp intense pain. That pain created even more fear, more muscular tightness, and less arousal, which continued to lead to pain with each thrust or attempt. They decided to stop because she was clearly very distressed, and he did not want to see her in so much pain. Each time they attempted vaginal penetrative sex after that was just as, if not more, difficult, scary, and painful for her, until she eventually would reflexively squirm away or push him off without there being any contact between their genitals.

Lifelong vs. Acquired

As for all sexual dysfunctions, it is important to distinguish between lifelong (sometimes also referred to as primary) and acquired (or secondary) GPPPD, in order to better understand the factors involved in its development and decide on the best approach to treat it. The term "lifelong" refers to situations where the person has always suffered from the condition for as long as they can remember, or since the beginning of their sexual life. This could reflect that the impact of predisposing and longstanding factors such as their upbringing and education may be stronger than that of current events. The majority of the clients I worked with in the Middle East who never had any sexual experience prior to marriage and were struggling to consummate their marriage would most likely fall under this category.

The term "acquired," however, means that the condition developed at a later time, potentially due to a specific event or trigger, or during a specific phase in that person's life. This could indicate that the specific events that may have triggered the issue may be more pertinent than the predisposing factors (though the predisposing factors need not be ignored). For example, if a client had a history of healthy and normal sex, but only started to experience pain or muscular tightness after a painful gynecological exam or childbirth, this scenario would fall under this category.

Generalized vs. Situational

For the sake of completeness, it could also be necessary to explain the difference between generalized and situational diagnoses. These terms are used for all sexual difficulties similarly to the "lifelong" and "acquired" adjectives. A diagnosis is "generalized" when the person experiences the difficulty in all and every situation(s). For example, a person with GPPPD would struggle with the same issue with different partners, and whether she is attempting to have vaginal penetrative sex or other activities such as inserting a tampon. A diagnosis is "situational," however, if she only experiences vaginismus with a particular partner or under specific circumstances (for example, she can insert a tampon but not have penetrative sex).

It is hard to determine whether or not the problem is "generalized" when the person is experiencing difficulties with the only sexual partner she has had. Having said that, the majority of the population I have worked with seem to have experienced "generalized" GPPPD as they have only had one partner, and either could not or have not attempted to insert a tampon or finger. Most of these women also had difficulties during gynecological exams.

Presentation of Penetration Disorders

Women have presented to me describing an inability to have sex and feeling confused about why something so "natural" could be so difficult. For some of them, penetration is literally impossible even when there is a physical attempt for the penis to enter the vagina, and many of the partners in this situation describe the sensation as "hitting a wall." It feels as if there is an obstacle preventing the penetration from happening, and sometimes feels like there is pressure in or around the vagina. For some women in this situation, they also experience pain that they may describe as a sharp pain, a burning pain, or even at times as if a knife or needle is poking them. Pain can be experienced even without penetration due to the friction or pressure caused by pushing the penis to enter the vagina, and the site is usually superficial around the vaginal opening. For women who are able to have vaginal penetrative sex and have dyspareunia, the pain could be superficial or deeper.

In other situations, which was a common presenting issue many of my previous clients brought into therapy, they were not even able to attempt penetration due to severe fear or a phobic response (which could be due to vaginismus or to vaginal penetration phobia). What tends to happen is that when the man approaches the woman to attempt penetration, she would either move away, push him off or block him from getting closer, lift her pelvis up in the air, and/or experience intense inner thigh tension and close her legs, thus preventing any attempt at penetration from occurring. Usually these are uncontrollable and automatic responses that are associated with her experiencing tremendous fear.

The majority of women who came to see me suffering from vaginismus were in their twenties, which may be because it is common in Arab or South-Asian countries for women to get married in their early twenties. In addition, I noticed that many of them tended to approach other aspects of their lives in a perfectionistic way and experience anxiety often, which is not surprising considering that the prevalence of depression and anxiety, especially specific phobia, was higher in women with vaginismus (Yildirim, Hacioglu, & Karaş, 2019; van Lankveld & Grotjohann, 2000; Farnam et al., 2014; Tetik et al., 2020). Most anxious people like to feel in control in order to soothe their anxiety, and so when they are put in a new situation, like the first time they are to have vaginal intercourse, they do not feel in control because it is unknown. Naturally, therefore, they involuntarily and automatically get scared. If they are also with an inexperienced partner, they might not feel safe enough to go through with it because they cannot trust that their partner is competent or will not unintentionally hurt them. It makes sense to me, as I believe her brain is protecting her from something it is perceiving as dangerous/unsafe by saying no or creating a fight/flight reaction.

Imagine you are going to climb a mountain that you have never been to before, and you have heard some positive and frightening things about it. You want to experience its beauty and adventure, but you are also a bit nervous about the novelty and potential difficulties. If you are going with an experienced guide who knows the mountain and seems confident, you are less likely to be nervous and more likely to feel safe enough to climb it with him despite your nervousness. Now imagine going with a first timer too, he has never been to that mountain, and is just as nervous. How would you feel? Unless you have the confidence to lead or are very comfortable with uncertainty and risk, I highly suspect you will either hesitate, or not want to go anymore, even though part of you might still wish to, or you might go but have a terrible experience filled with anxiety.

Very often women sought therapy with me because they had not been able to consummate their marriage after several months, and in a few cases even years. Many of them began treatment when they wished to conceive (Leiblum, 2007, p. 139) or when they started feeling the pressure of having children as per the expectations of their families or culture, which often happens a few months after the marriage. It seems that in Eastern cultures, where parents have more control over their children's sexual activity and time of procreation, couples tend to seek help sooner than in Western cultures, where the couples are more in control of their own sexual lives (Michetti et al., 2013). Many of my clients expressed feeling inadequate as they heard about other family members or friends getting pregnant shortly after getting married. Not to mention that the mere fact of not having been able to consummate their marriage also creates a sense of inadequacy and shame.

Sometimes there is a co-occurrence of dyspareunia, which may be the cause to begin with. If they attempted penetrative sex and it was painful, then that could lead to a fear of pain, which can then lead to experiencing vaginismus. It can be confusing to figure out what is causing what and what to treat first; the vaginismus or the dyspareunia? This is one of the reasons the new DSM-V merged vaginismus with dyspareunia into the GPPPD diagnosis. In these cases, I would try to look at the potential reasons for the pain. If I suspect that the pain is due to her fear and/or lack of arousal, then her fear and arousal are the real issue at hand that need to be addressed first. The reasoning is that once she feels more relaxed and aroused, she will not experience pain.

If she still experiences pain even after resolving her fears and arousal difficulties, then we may need to look at other potential causes for the pain and ways to manage it. In this situation, if the vaginismus or phobia is the reason for an unconsummated marriage or the lack of vaginal intercourse, then I would treat that first. Once the client has learned to be more relaxed and feels more in control, then I would work on resolving the pain. They very often come hand-in-hand anyway and the pain could potentially resolve itself once the vaginismus is treated. Similarly, if her fear of the pain that could be leading to her vaginismus is addressed, then that could potentially naturally eliminate the experience of pain.

Problems may sometimes present during genital examination (if the woman has attempted to get examined by her gynecologist) when the woman may show different degrees of distress. Some women lift their pelvis up as an automatic reflex, squirm and move away, or may even have severe adductor spasm, meaning their inner thighs tense up significantly, thus preventing anyone or anything from getting near their genital area. They often cannot tolerate even one finger being inserted into the vagina and show signs of immense distress. This could also be an indication of GPPPD in the absence of sexual activity – for example, in single or non-heterosexual women. Other signs of GPPPD could be difficulties inserting a tampon or a sex toy. Lastly, GPPPD is not limited to women who have not had children yet, but can also occur after childbirth.

Penetration Disorders in Arab, Middle-Eastern, and South-Asian Cultures

From my experience working with clients from the Middle East, Arab countries, or South Asia, the majority of female clients who presented with vaginismus or an unconsummated marriage were either in an arranged marriage or came from a strict religious or conservative background (Bokaie, Bostani Khalesi, & Yasini-Ardekani 2017; KSLatha et al., 2013). Performance anxiety, vaginismus, and premature ejaculation have been found to be some of the main causes behind unconsummated marriages in some of the conservative Middle-Eastern countries (Badran et al., 2006). An arranged marriage is when the bride and groom are selected not by the couple themselves, but by members of the community such as family members, often the parents, or even matchmakers, because they believe they are better able to select a suitable or satisfactory spouse than relying on the bride and groom (Batabyal & Beladi, 2002). Often in arranged marriages the couple may not have the opportunity to meet before the marriage, or they may meet in a group setting. From my observations and experience with the couples I've worked with who were in an arranged marriage, neither of the partners were forced to marry, and they are given the choice to refuse the partner. At the same time, there seems to be some family pressure regarding getting married by a certain age and within a certain social class, and it may feel very flattering for the woman to be "chosen" by the groom or groom's family. Therefore, one can imagine that in these situations, it could be difficult to refuse a potential spouse, and so while the woman may not have been forced to marry, she may not necessarily be fully ready for or wholeheartedly empowered about it. Of course, many women are, and so this is not to generalize to all cases of arranged marriages.

Though in some arranged marriages the couple has no interaction with each other prior to the marriage, either over the phone or in person, other couples who had an arranged marriage may have had some opportunities to get to know each other before marriage over the phone or in social group gatherings. I will still refer to these situations in the book as "arranged marriages" because the spouses usually marry someone from within the extended family or close community that has been chosen or approved of by their family. Despite them being able to meet each other and spend some time together prior to the marriage, the majority of the couples who worked with me had very little, if any, physical contact with each other before marriage. Sex before marriage is considered immoral in religious and conservative societies, and therefore these couples do not engage in any physical contact with each other that may be deemed as "sexual," such as kissing or touching of the body. Holding hands seems to be more acceptable, depending on the family values as well, but the majority of the time they will have not had any sexual contact with each other or more overt physical expressions of affection. It is not surprising then that having vaginal penetrative sex with a new husband can be petrifying if they have not had any sexual or physical contact with each other or anyone else before, and have received little or mostly negative information about sex.

From my observations with working with clients from traditional or religious cultures, the roles in arranged marriages also tend to conform to more traditional roles, with procreation being a priority, the woman being the primary caretaker of the children and family, and the man being the breadwinner. It seems that the majority of clients who presented to me in my practice fell in line with some of the findings around insufficient sexual education and traditional beliefs about virginity and the roles of the wife being significant factors associated with vaginismus in Arab-Muslim cultures (Zgueb et al., 2019). In addition, I noticed that attraction or passion are not emphasized or valued as much in arranged marriages, nor are they seen to be necessary for sexual relations, as sex is expected to be a natural consequence of marriage, and love is expected to develop as the couple deepens their relationship. Though decreasing in number, arranged marriages are quite common in the Middle East, Asia, and Africa (Rubio, 2014).

Modern love marriages differ from arranged marriages in that in love marriages, the partners are the ones who select each other (Batabyal & Beladi, 2002) and the marriage is usually based on mutual attraction and affection. Furthermore, couples who had a love marriage generally go through a dating process prior to the marriage where they get to know each other quite well, develop some emotional intimacy, and may have engaged in some form of sexual contact. In addition, though in some love marriages the male and female roles may still be traditional, the spouses tend to value love, connection, and passion as important parts of the marriage.

This is not to say that couples in arranged marriages do not love each other, or that love marriages are better than arranged marriages. Of course, many couples in arranged marriages do develop a deep loving connection, a high positive regard for each other, and intimacy. Love marriages have their fair share of challenges as well. One study in Pakistan, for example, found that couples in arranged marriages tend to be more vindictive and domineering, whereas couples in love marriages were more socially inhibited, non-assertive, and intrusive (Akhtar et al., 2017). Considering that many of my clients were in arranged marriages, and that in arranged marriages the couple tends to have fewer opportunities to develop their sexual relationship progressively prior to or even at the start of the marriage, I think it is important for professionals working with clients from these types of background to understand where they are coming from in order to best support them.

Recognizing that the passion or sexual desire that exists in love marriages may not be the same in some arranged marriages means that, when working with couples in arranged marriages, we may need to get more creative in helping them develop intimacy and create sufficient arousal and interest in sex for them to have a positive experience. We also need to pay attention to our own transference and judgments of what we believe is "right" in a marriage and address any of our feelings about arranged marriages that may be affecting our work. Of course, we therapists always strive to work with clients in an ethical manner and want to ensure that our approach is aligned with our professional and ethical values, and so we may need to modify our approach in a way that can help promote intimacy and arousal within the traditions and framework of an arranged marriage. If clients do not value passion as much as we do, and believe that love and intimacy develop with experience and time together, then we may need to tailor our work so that we are supporting them through developing that instead of pushing our own beliefs about passion onto them.

Case Examples

Shamsa, a 21-year-old woman from the UAE recently married her cousin, Khalid, who is 24 years old, after being encouraged by her family. Like many couples within their community, they did not have a lot of time to get to know each other (emotionally, mentally, and physically) prior to the marriage. They did not spend quality time or time alone with each other in person prior to the marriage, but had only had conversations over the phone to get to know each other. The only opportunities they had to meet each other in person were during certain holidays with the family, which involved mostly formal interactions and conversations between them. Neither of them had any consensual sexual experience or contact with any partner prior to the marriage or with each other, let alone any exploration of their own sexuality with themselves. Shortly after the marriage, the families started to enquire about when they were going to get pregnant and started to suspect they were having problems when there was no sign of pregnancy after two or three months.

Like many other couples in their situation, they were too ashamed to share with their families that they were experiencing sexual difficulties, and so they suffered in silence for a while. In addition to their own feelings of inadequacy and disappointment, they endured many interrogations and speeches from their parents pressuring them about having children. Though they eventually sought professional help to address their issues, other couples in similar situations are sometimes advised by their families to get a divorce due to not being able to consummate their marriage. Sharing such issues with the family can feel very shameful and embarrassing for the couple and may at times make it even more challenging for the woman to find another suitable husband in the future if word gets out about her difficulties. At the same time, other couples may just keep this secret from their families and friends and stay in an unconsummated marriage for several years until they seek help from me. I suspect there are other couples who either eventually get a divorce or stay in the unconsummated marriage together feeling quite inadequate and lacking intimacy.

Another client, Maysa, on the other hand, shared most of her personal information with her mother. Maysa came from a less religious family and culture, and yet personally held a lot of shame and taboos around sex. She had no problem discussing her issues with her mother who was very supportive. In addition, she was in a love marriage with a man she met on her own and personally chose to

> be with, without any pressure or arrangement from the families. Maysa's case is to show that not all women who suffer from GPPPD (and certainly not all the women I worked with) are in an arranged marriage.

Many women (and men) come to see me months or even years after being married and not being able to consummate their marriage, feeling inadequate and worthless, as if what they were experiencing should not be happening and that it was a reflection of their own personal failure. That makes me very sad, as I believe that it is only natural for a woman's body to be protecting itself from doing something that does not feel safe, and it is absolutely understandable for her body not to feel safe engaging in an experience she may have learned could be painful with someone she has not developed a secure relationship with yet. Sure, it should not take years for a couple to consummate their marriage, and the fact that it does indicates that something needs to be resolved, but what I am saying is that sex is complex, and the body is trying to send a message by rejecting it. *There is a function behind the dysfunction.*

Women in arranged marriages or from very conservative backgrounds are expected to go from no sexual experience and very little connection with the man before marriage, to engaging in one of the most intimate and scary things a woman can do for the first time without any difficulty. I find that completely unhelpful and unrealistic. I believe we should be re-educating people and setting a more realistic expectation; specifically, that newly married couples who come from a religious or conservative background and have not had much time to get to know each other or explore their sexuality should spend weeks, or even months (depending on the couple's needs), bonding, going on dates, touching, learning about each other, and exploring each other's sexuality gradually and in a safe way, before even attempting vaginal penetrative sex.

Going back to the example of climbing a mountain, imagine that you have never climbed a mountain before, and you have little, if any, skills around hiking or climbing, and you are then pressured into climbing one of the toughest mountains around. It may not be as challenging in reality, but you have heard many stories about it being difficult and scary, and that some people have gotten injured while climbing it. Add to the mix the fact that you are expected to climb it with someone you have not fully developed a deeply trusting relationship with yet, and has little skill or experience climbing difficult mountains as well. That sounds scary, and I believe it would be completely understandable for you to feel scared. I also believe that expecting you to climb that specific mountain when you have not established the skills necessary to climb it is counterproductive and potentially harmful. What I am suggesting, instead, is for you to start with smaller and easier hills, mountains, and terrains, to build more confidence, skill, experience, and trust, until you feel more ready to tackle that mountain.

Additionally, what often happens is that many people are not aware of what vaginismus is and how to treat it, so they keep attempting intercourse in the same manner, leading to the same difficulties, and ultimately reinforcing the fears and feelings of disappointment and inadequacy, until it either becomes very severe, or they just stop trying altogether. And this is how sometimes years end up passing by before they seek help. And if they have attempted to resolve the issue sooner, very often they were not provided with the right professional help, did not have access to a sexual or mental health professional, and may even have been prescribed muscle relaxants or been told by doctors to just "relax." This brings me to another very crucial message I am trying to send out there: that people need to address their difficulties and fears sooner rather than later, and get the right help. The longer they wait, the more complex the cycle becomes, and the longer it might take to treat it.

By "the right help" I mean consulting professionals who have been specifically trained in working with sexual dysfunctions, and, ideally, who have a background in psychotherapy as well. Most of the time clients consult gynecologists, not sex therapists (Zgueb et al., 2019). Consulting a gynecologist may be helpful at times, but it is not always sufficient, as unfortunately many medical doctors do not have adequate training in this area. In addition, they tend to address the issue purely and sometimes inappropriately from a physical standpoint, thus ignoring and potentially exacerbating the emotional and psychological barriers. I have seen my fair share of women who have had their hymens surgically removed (hymenectomy) because their gynecologist believed that their "tight" hymens were the reason behind their sexual difficulties. Lo and behold, these same women appeared back in my office a few weeks or months after their procedures.

Clearly the issue was never about the hymen, but the woman's psychological and emotional states were not sufficiently taken into consideration. Therefore, imagine being taken through unnecessary surgical procedures, in the area that you already hold very negative and scary beliefs about, only to find yourself in the same, if not worse, position afterwards. For the sake of accuracy and transparency, I have had one client who had a hymenectomy that she claimed did help her consummate her marriage, though she somehow still found herself in my office. Of course, it is possible for some women that going through a procedure like this and believing that their hymen is more open and "loose" could be just what they need to feel more relaxed and confident. I would not be able to determine how many women successfully resolved their issues by going through this procedure as they would not show up in my practice. What I do know is that many women who had had a hymenectomy still sought therapy with me because it did not help.

It is important for us clinicians to assess whether or not what the client is experiencing is just part of the "normal" acclimating journey of learning to become sexual with a new partner for the first time, or whether it is time for professional help to be involved. As I mentioned earlier, it is understandable to need some time to be able to have vaginal penetrative sex if they are recently married and have never had sex before, and so it is not necessary to panic, or even potentially treat it, if they are experiencing difficulties in the first month or two. However, if they are not finding that their fears or difficulties are decreasing with more attempts and the passage of time, or if their attempts are, in fact, becoming more difficult, or their difficulties persist for several months, then I strongly recommend that they consult a professional.

If they are concerned in any way or need some support, I believe it is important for them to talk to someone they trust; their qualified doctor or therapist, a compassionate family member or friend, do some research, and look for trained professionals such as sex therapists as soon as possible. Even if they seek out therapy in the first two to six months, which technically might not qualify as a diagnosis of GPPPD if it has not been persistent for at least six months, I believe it would still be helpful to provide them with the right education, information, and tools to prevent the development of GPPPD and help make their journey easier and more enjoyable. In fact, I wish people would give themselves the opportunity to seek professional help sooner more often, as this could save them much pain, time, and money down the line.

The number of women I treated for vaginismus who come from liberal or non-traditional cultures was much lower, but that does not mean that only women from conservative or religious cultures suffer from vaginismus. Unconsummated marriages occur in Western cultures as well, whether due to erectile dysfunction, premature ejaculation, or vaginismus (Michetti et al., 2013). My observation, however, was that women who came from more liberal backgrounds who have had sexual experience prior to the marriage or who have spent enough time creating a secure and deeper relationship with their partner, presented to me with acquired or secondary vaginismus (such as after a traumatic gynecological exam or a painful experience), or had other individual or relational factors that contributed significantly. I have seen far fewer non-traditional women with lifelong/primary vaginismus (vaginismus that has always been present).

Case Example

One example of acquired/secondary vaginismus is a young European couple who came to see me after months of experiencing difficult penetrative sex. They had been married a couple of years and had been sexually active and successfully able to have vaginal penetrative sex with each other even prior to the marriage. However, in recent months the wife had started to experience an uncontrollable fear, tensing of her pelvic muscles, and painful sex. As we explored some of the potential factors, we identified that she had had a traumatic and painful gynecological exam not too long before all of her difficulties started. Of course, there were other factors as well, such as some shame associated with sex and a discomfort from both the husband and wife regarding openly discussing their sexual feelings and preferences with each other, but the main precipitating event that triggered her vaginismus was the painful gynecological exam. This is different from women who have never had any sexual experience and have struggled with vaginismus since the beginning of their sexual attempts with their partner (lifelong vaginismus). Nevertheless, I would follow similar guidelines in the treatment in both cases.

Maysa, who was mentioned earlier, was somewhat sexually active with her husband prior to the marriage, and enjoyed sensual touch and giving and receiving manual stimulation, but had not had vaginal penetrative sex before marriage. They had a high interest in sex before the marriage and shortly after, until the difficulties they faced with penetration started to impact their desires. She seemed to be more relaxed about sexual contact before the marriage, and once vaginal intercourse became "acceptable" or expected (after marriage), her anxiety about sex showed up significantly. This is not uncommon — many women (and men for that matter) show a lot of interest and arousal during sexual experiences that do not involve penetration or performance, and yet when vaginal penetrative sex is anticipated or attempted, they display and experience a lot of anxiety, and as a result, less arousal and interest. Maysa's case falls into the category of lifelong vaginismus, and yet she was sexually active (excluding vaginal penetrative sex) prior to the marriage, thus showing that not all women with vaginismus or GPPPD had no sexual experience prior to attempting to consummate their marriage.

Although, technically, vaginismus is a sexual dysfunction that interferes with vaginal penetrative sex in particular, I believe that other sexual difficulties have many similarities with vaginismus and can be treated in a similar fashion. If a client experiences shame, significant discomfort, or anxiety around sex, or difficulties around her sexual enjoyment and arousal, then many of the exercises and concepts in this book may help her overcome these negative feelings and attitudes and change her sexual experiences for the better. The main point is that the client does not need to have difficulties with penetration or consummating her marriage per se for this book to be useful and helpful to the clinician or client reading it.

Therapeutic Interventions for Clinician and Client

Generally speaking, the management of vaginismus requires a multidimensional multidisciplinary approach, and the treatment should be tailored for each individual woman and partner. The partner's involvement is encouraged but it is up to the client to choose whether and when to involve her partner. Most of my female clients have started the process of therapy on their own; as they progress through the individual exercises, and when they have gained sufficient confidence to start the couple's exercises, they involve their partner in the sessions. This sequence has been my preferred approach in terms of involving the partner in the exercises. Nonetheless, I strongly encourage the client to share her journey with her partner in terms of her growth, learning, progressions, and challenges, in order to build more connection and understanding. This has been what the majority of the clients I have worked with have done and it seemed to have worked out quite well for them. It is also absolutely acceptable and wonderful if the partner wants to be involved in the process from the beginning, as some relational factors could be contributing and addressed as well.

The concept behind my method for treating vaginismus is an integration of the cognitive and behavioral approaches usually used to treat it, in addition to a significant emphasis on the intra- and inter-personal emotional and psychological work. The behavioral treatment is generally based on principles of problem-oriented short-term therapy with practical and desensitization exercises. It is necessary to maintain a gradual approach in overcoming this difficulty that includes education, homework assignments, and cognitive therapy. The insights and suggestions provided in this book are based on my clinical experience of working with clients. Although my experience has been mainly with women from the Middle East or South Asia, most of the steps and theories discussed in this book are applicable to women from other cultures.

In summary, the woman learns to reframe some of her unrealistic beliefs about sex while she undergoes, in parallel, gradual exposure therapy by practicing gently and progressively introducing trainers of increasing size (can be fingers, tampons, or vaginal trainers, but I usually recommend using her own fingers). It is very important for the woman to be in total control of the process, which gives her great confidence. This is why I highly recommend that she starts with the solo exercises (in Chapter 5), and then progresses to introducing the fingers with her partner only after she has mastered the first stages. *I also strongly advise that she and her partner refrain from attempting vaginal penetrative sex during this process, until after they have completed the solo and partner exercises.* The gradual exposure process also involves progressions of non-sexual followed by more sexual touch that the couple will experience together. Once she is ready, she can attempt the insertion of the penis into the vagina with her in control of and guiding the process (this will all be discussed in more detail in later chapters). I also recommend that she keeps a journal of her experiences throughout. This will help to keep track of her thoughts, feelings, exercises, and progress, and better identify what worked, what did not, and what can be modified.

I have formulated the following guidelines based on my clinical experience working with many women and couples who were not able to consummate their marriage, in addition to all my education, training, knowledge, and intuition. The main concepts behind my method are similar to other treatments and self-help books for vaginismus, but the main differences are, firstly, that this comprises a more holistic approach addressing the mental, physical, and emotional layers, and secondly, that it is based on my experience with religious cultures, and so might be more helpful to women from such backgrounds (though this can definitely help any woman struggling with the issue at hand). It is important for me to note that not all women need to go through all of the stages in this book to overcome their difficulties. Some women may just require a few sessions of psychoeducation and dilation exercises, and this may be sufficient for them to be able to attempt vaginal intercourse successfully. By no means, therefore, am I suggesting that this treatment approach is better than others, or that only focusing on the progressive desensitization/gradual exposure therapy and dilation is bad, wrong, or insufficient. What I am offering is a program that does not just address the muscular or physical component of the issue, but also helps instill more confidence within the client and more connection within the relationship. This may be necessary for some women, and for others it may simply be more desirable because it feels more aligned with their personal and relationship goals.

If you are a woman struggling with GPPPD and reading this in order to attempt to resolve it, my recommendation is to read the whole book, without skipping any steps or chapters, as some things that are written later in the book can be helpful even if you have made significant progress at earlier stages of the treatment. Since GPPPD can be complex issues, I cannot guarantee that the book is going to be enough to treat them but hopefully many of you will find that it is.

This book was also written under the assumption that the woman is attracted to her partner or WANTS to have sex with him. If she is not attracted to him or has no desire to be intimate with him (or is not sure), then I strongly recommend that she seeks counseling for that first. It is common for women and their partners to lose interest in having sex or start avoiding sex after a period of unsuccessful and stressful attempts, but that is different than not desiring her partner to begin with. If she is avoiding sex because it has been stressful, but she very much wanted to be intimate with her partner in the beginning, you can still work with her following the guidelines of the book and hopefully her interest in sex will return once she overcomes some of her fears, gains more confidence, and creates more intimacy. If, however, she has never been interested in sex with her partner or has never been attracted to him (or even feels repulsed by him), then I highly recommend that she seeks counseling to address that specific issue instead.

I think one perspective to keep in mind when discussing or working with low desire is the work of Rosemary Basson, who offers a revised version of the traditional notion that sexual function and response in women follows a sequential model of different stages starting with sexual desire (libido), sexual arousal (excitement), orgasm, and satisfaction. For example, instead of viewing sexual desire as a linear concept that happens spontaneously and triggers arousal, one may see desire and arousal as co-occurring and reinforcing each other (Basson et al., 2004). It is therefore important to take into consideration the social and contextual factors that may inhibit or augment the client's receptivity to sexual stimuli.

Some women are very resistant to treatment and may require skillful couples therapy or long-term individual therapy – vaginismus in such cases is probably the presenting symptom of a more complex sexual or relationship problem. If the woman has attempted the necessary steps through this or other self-help books and has not made any progress after a few weeks, or deeper issues have been triggered, then I would suggest that she pursues psychotherapy or couples therapy to address more potentially complex emotional or relational factors (for example, sexual trauma, or not feeling connected to the partner). As mentioned before, and will be explored further later, there may be an underlying cause for the condition.

2 Psychological and Emotional Factors

The first step that is crucial for change is to provide education and correct any misinformation about sexual functioning, the genitals, and the client's body. This is part of the cognitive aspect of therapy as we aim to question, challenge, and change the unrealistic beliefs about female and male sexuality. Cognitive behavioral therapy is useful to reduce anxiety and fear (phobia) by challenging and reducing the negative thoughts and beliefs associated with sex. In a retrospective study conducted on 100 women in Saudi Arabia who suffered from vaginal penetration phobia and could not consummate the marriage, it was found that misinformation about sex or insufficient sex education was one of the main contributing factors in the development of these women's fears (Muammar et al., 2015) (for women looking for sexual health information in Arabic, I found the Instagram account @mauj.me to be a great resource).

Therefore, before the client starts practicing the behavioral exercises to help her explore and progressively desensitize her body, I believe it is necessary to first guide her in questioning and possibly modifying some of her misguided expectations and beliefs about sex. The reasoning behind this is that our beliefs have a direct impact on our feelings and actions, which in turn affect our experience. If, therefore, her beliefs about sex are unrealistic or negative, she will engage in sex accordingly and potentially have a negative experience, which will then lead to feelings of inadequacy, disappointment, and anxiety. Those negative feelings will then reinforce her dysfunctional beliefs, thus maintaining this negative vicious cycle.

For example, if she believes that a penis is too large to fit in a vagina, or inversely, that the vagina is too small to accommodate a penis, then she will most likely feel very scared when attempting PIV sex as she will anticipate pain. When she is afraid, she is most likely not going to be aroused or lubricated enough, and her pelvic muscles may tighten up, which will inevitably make vaginal penetrative sex painful or impossible. This will then reinforce her beliefs that her vagina is too small, and that sex is painful, which will lead to more anxiety about sex. Next time there is an attempt at PIV sex, she will most likely feel even more scared, and possibly avoid sex, or engage in it and have yet another stressful or painful experience. You can see where this is going. Even though to us clinicians, it may be obvious that the vagina is not too small to

DOI: 10.4324/9781003129172-2

accommodate a penis, as it is a muscle that expands and can even accommodate a whole baby, for a client with inaccurate or incomplete sex education, that may very well be an unrealistic belief that we would need to help her shift through the course of the treatment. Some of the most common unrealistic beliefs about sex that are relevant to GPPPD are discussed later.

In addition to providing accurate and realistic information about sex, part of reframing sex for the client happens through helping her gain a better understanding of how she feels about her body and sex, how much shame, guilt, and disgust she holds around them, and what kinds of experiences may have contributed to those feelings. Increasing her self-awareness around these factors, while working through the behavioral exercises in parallel (in Chapter 5), can help the client shift her attitude toward her genitals and sexuality. Furthermore, part of the healing journey for the client should also involve processing any trauma or sexual abuse she may have experienced in her childhood or adulthood. In a nutshell, what I have found to be helpful is to support the client through processing and reframing any misconceptions about and shame around sex, healing any sexual trauma, while at the same time, engaging in behavioral exercises that will experientially shift her relationship with her body.

Expectations Around Sex

Having realistic expectations about her first sexual experience can tremendously help the client have a positive experience. Many women fantasize about their first time being a deeply romantic and passionate experience. On the other hand, for women who learned that they may bleed severely, or that it will be painful and potentially traumatic, they most likely will dread their first time – imagining it to be a scary and excruciatingly painful experience. The reality is that for many people, the first time they have sex is awkward and possibly uncomfortable. That does not mean that it will not be enjoyable or meaningful, but that it is completely natural for the first time, or even the first few experiences, to feel awkward and mechanical as the couple gradually get to know each other's sexuality and feel more comfortable with their bodies and each other. The first time may involve some pain, but it should not be unbearable, and it should not be so dreadful.

One of the most fundamental pieces of education every woman (and man) should know, is that sex is a complex experience. Though many people treat it like a "natural" animalistic instinct that should be easy, it is in fact much more complex than animals' sexuality. For many people, it is not just a simple mechanical phenomenon that is completed purely through physical stimulation and penetration. Nonetheless, it is quite common for women and men who come from religious or conservative backgrounds to still believe that a woman (and man) should be able to immediately have PIV sex after marriage without time and opportunities to get more emotionally and physically intimate with the partner first.

Psychological and Emotional Factors

In addition, it is often a common belief that the emotional and mental components are not important, whereas in reality, they are crucial. So crucial that some of my male clients who suffered from erectile difficulties were sometimes still unable to achieve or maintain erections even when they took prescription medications that are meant to help them get an erection. This may suggest that what they were truly suffering from was sexual performance anxiety as opposed to organic erectile dysfunction, and that the psychological components of anxiety can lead to physical difficulties. As explained in the previous chapter, fear of pain or vaginal penetration can lead to pelvic muscle contractions, thus contributing to vaginismus and/or painful sex, which is another indication of how the psychological and emotional factors can significantly impact one's sexual experience.

Taking all of that into consideration, when all three components (mental, physical, and emotional) are functioning in a healthy and harmonious way, one can have a fulfilling and enjoyable sexual experience. This does not mean that all three areas must be at an optimal level to have a successful sexual experience; some people are still able to have pleasurable sex without one or some of these factors. And for other people, sex may possibly be a less sensual and meaningful experience if one of the key components is missing for them. What I am focusing on in this book, however, is how to have sexual intimacy without fear and pain. I believe this is of the utmost importance and yet many women either do not realize it is possible to have sex without pain, or do not prioritize their needs, often because they believe they should be having sex regardless of the pain.

Sex should not be painful if the woman is sufficiently aroused, lubricated, and relaxed. Therefore, worrying about the pain is usually unfounded and mostly based on myths and unrealistic expectations. Fear of pain will often lead to lower arousal and difficulty achieving a relaxed state, which can then lead to sex being more painful. It is thus crucial for a woman to have the right knowledge and appropriate experience in order to be sufficiently relaxed, aroused, and prepared for sex.

The terms arousal and desire are often used interchangeably. However, though they reinforce each other, they are quite different. While desire represents one's interest in sex, arousal is the physiological and psychological response to sex. When a person is aroused, there is increased blood flow to the genital area (labia, clitoris, and vagina), and vaginal lubrication. These changes help prepare the person for sex. The person feels "turned on" or "excited," and when arousal builds up, orgasm can occur at its climax with appropriate stimulation. Many factors can lead to arousal; the sexual arousal circuit set out in Figure 2.1 describes in more depth how each of those factors contribute and what is required for sufficient arousal and connected sex (I believe this arousal circuit is based on the works of Dr. Elizabeth Stanley). Of course, the degree to which each of these components negatively or positively affects a person's arousal varies from one person to another.

24 *Psychological and Emotional Factors*

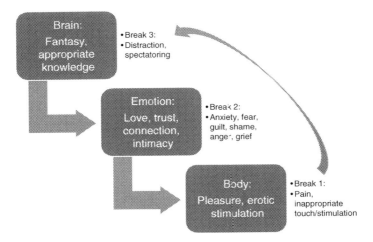

Figure 2.1 Sexual arousal circuit.

Physical: there has to be sufficient and appropriate physical stimulation for there to be sufficient arousal and pleasure. If the stimulation is not performed in a way that pleasures the individual, or if it is painful or uncomfortable, that could create a break in the sexual arousal circuit. In other words, one needs to be touched in a way that gives pleasure, and if, on the other hand, sex is painful, uncomfortable, or actually unpleasurable for any reason, physical or psychological arousal may not happen.

Mental: one must be present and focused on the body and on the experience to be able to fully enjoy it. If one is distracted (by other irrelevant thoughts, anxiety, or other external stimuli), or spectatoring (when you feel you are watching yourself or evaluating your performance during the experience rather than being present in it), then that could create a break in the sexual arousal circuit.

Emotional: one must feel connected, loving, relaxed, and trusting/safe to be able to let go and give and receive. If there are trust issues or emotional blocks such as shame, anxiety, anger, or lack of connection, this could cause a break in the cycle.

Myths and Unhealthy Beliefs About Sex

In addition to having realistic expectations about her first sexual experience, having the right information about sex in general can be very helpful for the client to engage in sex in a healthy and positive way. Many of us grew up hearing stories or being told pieces of information that are not true, thus creating myths about sex that negatively impact our future relationships. I believe that it is therefore crucial for us therapists to help the client become aware of those faulty beliefs and correct them, especially when she holds a lot of shame and fear around sex. Below are some of the common myths and unrealistic beliefs about sex, many of which are frequently seen in women with GPPPD or vaginal penetration phobia. I would like to highlight that many of these beliefs are also widely held in the general public, as well as by people with other sexual difficulties, and so exploring them could also be helpful when working with other types of sexual dysfunctions or sexual shame in general.

Having Sex for the First Time Is Going to Be Painful

Many women fear their first night as a married couple, mainly due to the anticipation that sex is expected and will be extremely painful. Vaginal penetrative sex can be painful the first time (or few times), but it should not be unbearable or excruciating. Sex can be very painful if the woman is not relaxed or aroused enough. Therefore, if she is feeling safe, connected, and enough attention is paid to get her psychologically and physically turned on, then it should not be very painful. If she is not relaxed or does not feel ready for PIV sex, then I would strongly suggest that the couple puts it on hold and focuses more on non-penetrative intimate and sexual expression and getting to know each other's bodies by kissing, petting, giving and receiving sensual touch, or pleasuring each other manually or orally.

I definitely encourage newlyweds who have not had sexual experience to take a lot of time touching each other and seducing each other in the beginning of their marriage until they both feel ready for vaginal intercourse. Therefore, when working with a client who holds this common belief, it is important to educate her on the inaccuracy of this belief and what factors could potentially lead to her experiencing a lot of pain. If she is equipped with better information, then she and her husband can approach PIV sex in a way to ensure that she is feeling relaxed and aroused and reduce the likelihood of her experiencing pain.

The Hymen Breaking Means Losing Your Virginity

Many people believe that the hymen is a flat piece of tissue that covers the vagina and "breaks" during vaginal intercourse. If that were the case, then girls would not be able to menstruate before losing their virginity as there would be a barrier preventing the blood from exiting. I find it quite surprising to see how many people are misinformed about this particular subject. I, for one, can relate to that! The reality is that the hymen is a fringe of tissue around the vaginal opening (like a scrunchy) that stretches during vaginal penetrative sex and other non-sexual activities (such as athletic activities), but does not "break." Some girls have very little tissue to begin with, and not all girls bleed during their first sexual encounter. Therefore, defining virginity only by the "breaking" of the hymen is very limiting and does not reflect the reality as the hymen can be stretched without PIV sex.

The shape of the hymen is not a sign of virginity, and despite some countries still conducting "virginity tests," there is no medical examination that can accurately assess whether or not someone has had sex. Virginity is a very personal thing; it is whatever the person thinks it is. For some, it has more of an emotional connotation, not just a physical stretching of the hymen. When working with clients who view virginity in such a traditional sense, I find that it is pertinent to work on shifting that view to a more up-to-date and personal one, as the concept of virginity has become a very profound and heavy one for the client, that may create immense pressure on "losing it."

The topic of "virginity" is a significant one to note, especially in conservative or traditional types of societies or families, as huge importance is placed on a woman remaining a virgin until marriage. Preserving a woman's virginity until marriage is valued to the extent that some gynecologists in some of these countries will not even agree to examine a woman if she is not married, which, as you can imagine, not only reinforces the myths around virginity and the hymen, but also poses certain health risks as some women may be suffering from medical problems such as cervical cancer that are left untreated. One of my clients in Saudi Arabia even told me that tampons are not readily available in supermarkets, and shared a story of a friend of hers who had to undergo a hysterectomy through the abdomen as opposed to through the vagina because she was not married. These examples reflect some of the more indirect and yet significant ways the "hymen myth" may be affecting women. Additionally, some gynecologists offer hymenoplasty surgery (a surgical procedure to "repair" or "reconstruct" the hymen) to women who have (secretly) had vaginal intercourse prior to marriage and want to be "revirginized" for the wedding night to show their "purity."

For a girl growing up in a culture that emphasizes the necessity for the woman to be a virgin, she learns that, if she is not a virgin, she will not find someone to marry her, she may be ostracized, rejected from her family and/or society, shamed, and maybe even threatened or harmed in extreme cases. The hymen myths and misconceptions are greatly upheld in patriarchal societies, where virginity is emphasized and only to be lost when consummating a marriage (Cinthio, 2015). It is not surprising, then, that it would be extremely difficult for her to "lose" or let go of the one precious thing she was continuously told to preserve, especially to a man she has not had sufficient opportunity to build trust and connection with yet. Considering the significance that society places on the hymen and virginity being associated with a woman's purity or social acceptance, it would be valuable to support the client in challenging some of the myths about the hymen, reframing what the hymen really is about, and what virginity means to her on an emotional and personal level (Christianson & Eriksson, 2013).

Women Bleed the First Time They Have Sex

That is true sometimes, but not always. And if the woman does not bleed, it does not mean she is not a virgin (virginity here defined as not having had vaginal intercourse). Some women whose hymens have been stretched due to athletic or other types of activities that may stretch the hymen might not bleed much or at all the first time. Additionally, as mentioned previously, some women have less hymen tissue to begin with. This is a particularly important myth to bust when working with women with penetration difficulties or vaginal penetration phobia because the expectation that they may bleed significantly is related to the fears that sex will be painful or that their external or internal genitalia might be damaged or ruptured.

Sex Should Be Natural and Spontaneous – Asking for It Spoils It

The reality is that sex is sometimes spontaneous, and sometimes it is not. Especially after being in a committed relationship for a long period of time, the initial excitement of the novelty can wear off, and it may require more creativity and conscious efforts to keep the spark alive. If the client believes that sex should always be spontaneous, then she is setting herself and her marriage up for disappointment. In fact, very often in long-term relationships, and for many women, desire is responsive, and comes after some sort of connection, physical contact, or highly erotic cues and context. For example, the person may not feel a spontaneous urge for or interest in sex, but might get into the mood after kissing her partner, having a romantic or fun evening with them, dressing up in sexy clothes, or dancing sensually. Many people, particularly women, are more naturally responsive rather than spontaneous in their sexual desires, even if they find their partner to be very attractive (Basson et al., 2004) (Emily Nagoski's book, "*Come As You Are*," 2015, is a great resource for this topic).

Though this myth is not necessarily always directly relevant to penetration difficulties, I believe it is still important to challenge and change it because some of these women do not feel spontaneously interested in sex in the beginning of their marriage due to their fears and the insufficient level of intimacy they have established with their husbands. If we are able to validate their experience and aid them into recognizing that it is possible to build sexual desire and arousal, that can help lift some of the guilt and sense of inadequacy experienced by them and give them a more realistic platform to work from.

All Physical Contact Must Lead to Sex

The problem with this one is that physical touch can then become associated with anxiety or stress. Let us say that one way the husband expresses love is by kissing or touching the client, and that is all he wants to do sometimes; however, the wife might think that by kissing her, he is initiating sex. What can happen is that if she is not in the mood for sex, she will feel anxious and pressured to have sex, and will either start a sexual relation out of duty, or reject the husband's kisses and touch. Neither of those scenarios ends well, as the former will lead to a build-up of resentment and associating sex with a feeling of obligation, and the latter will lead to the husband feeling rejected and hurt, and less likely to show physical affection in the future. Of course, it is also possible that she may start to get aroused and enjoy the sex after she gets into it, and so it may not always end badly. Nonetheless, I believe that this way of thinking can end up limiting a couple's intimacy and contributing to the anxiety or pressure around sex and physical contact.

Sometimes it is just about kissing, or touching, or holding each other, without any sexual activity. And sometimes there could be a build-up that leads to some sexual contact but not PIV sex or orgasm, or just orgasm and not penetration. Any and all of these scenarios are just as valid as vaginal penetrative sex, and it is important for us to teach clients to expand their definitions of intimacy to incorporate more physical affection and emotional intimacy with less pressure. I will expand on this as it is so important to have physical affection that is not sexual to increase emotional intimacy.

Masturbation Is Bad for You

Let me just clarify firstly that I am speaking from a scientific and professional perspective, so I am leaving religion and personal values out of the discussion. This is, of course, a personal choice, but from the scientific point of view, masturbation is healthy. Firstly, it helps the individual learn about and understand how their body responds and how they feel pleasure so that they can experience pleasure and share it with their partner. Exploring one's own body and learning to give themself pleasure can be empowering and can help create a more positive body image. Secondly, orgasms are a healthy way for the body to release certain "feel-good" chemicals in the brain, and can help one relax. Thirdly, it is healthy for a man's prostate to ejaculate on a regular basis. Once again, though this specific subject might not be clearly involved in the client's penetration issues, it is just another negative belief about sex that exacerbates the shame she already has about sex, pleasure, and the genitals. Therefore, I believe it may be helpful to explore these themes, provide her with more accurate information, and normalize self-pleasure so that she can adopt more healthy views.

Some people have concerns around compulsive sexual behaviors (such as masturbation). Though I do not like to label such issues as "sex addictions," if the person feels they are not in control of these behaviors, and these compulsive behaviors are causing them distress or disrupting their lives, then I would encourage them to discuss this with a professional counselor or therapist. As I mentioned before, self-pleasuring is not harmful in and of itself, and if anything, has many physical and psychological benefits. However, at times, these compulsive sexual behaviors may reflect deeper emotional issues such as loneliness and/or difficulties with emotional regulation, and so it may be helpful to learn more effective self-soothing strategies and address some of the emotional components underneath.

Men Should Know Everything About Sex, Especially How to Pleasure a Woman

It is both the man's and the woman's responsibilities to learn about sex in terms of gathering information from reliable sources, exploring their own bodies and sexualities, and communicating with each other about their preferences and boundaries. Every man and woman is different, therefore even though there are some methods or guidelines that work for many, each individual has specific needs and ways that stimulate him/her in the right way. It is up to both of them to firstly know their own bodies, desires, and boundaries, and secondly, to communicate this with each other and explore together so they can learn how to fulfill each other's sexual desires.

This myth would be useful to address in women and couples who are struggling with penetrative sex, or sex in general, to give the woman more permission and power to familiarize herself with her sexuality and to communicate more openly with her partner. This will also help lift the pressure off of the man needing to take complete charge of the situation. When the woman expects the man to be the only or main person in the relationship responsible for good sex, not only could this lead to disappointment and resentment when he does not perform according to her expectations, but it could also remove her sense of power in sex. When she has less power when it comes to sex, she could experience less confidence and more fear.

Having Sex Means Having Vaginal Intercourse

The word sex encompasses so much, and yet is so loosely and widely used to indicate just PIV sex. Unfortunately, viewing sex in such a limited manner can lead to difficulties because it adds a lot of pressure on performance and inaccurately "measuring" how much sex a couple has. For example, if a man or woman has some anxiety or discomfort with vaginal penetrative sex, or is not particularly in the mood for it, but would like to be intimate with their partner in other ways, defining sex as PIV sex limits that possibility and puts pressure on them to only have vaginal intercourse. The only two choices they feel they have are to either have "sex" or say no (or make up an excuse). The first will ultimately lead to resentment and associating sex with pressure and expectations, and the second will lead to more rejection and distance. On the other hand, if people expanded their views of sex and considered other forms of seduction, eroticism, pleasure, touch, or even flirtatious texting or words as sex, they would not feel pressure to engage in PIV sex, and would instead feel safe and close and more open to playfulness.

I feel that this is a crucial definition to shift when working with couples with sexual difficulties, especially for women with fear of, or pain during, penetration. Defining sex as only vaginal intercourse while experiencing pain and/or fear of sex can put tremendous pressure on sex and create immense anxiety and guilt. If the woman believes her only option for intimacy or sex is vaginal penetrative sex and yet she is deeply afraid of it, that can put her in a huge predicament and can lead to her feeling very inadequate and worthless. And if sex is painful to her, then she might force herself to endure the pain during sex to avoid disappointment, thus reinforcing the pain cycle and making her go through unnecessary suffering. One of the definitions of sex that I really liked was offered in the book "*Mind The Gap*" by Dr. Karen Gurney (which I highly recommend), who said "Sex is any physical or psychological act that uses your body or mind for sexual pleasure or expression" (2020, p. 102).

If You Cannot Orgasm, You Are not Normal

There are many misconceptions about a woman's orgasm, and one of them is that women should orgasm through PIV sex. We can partially blame the media and television for this, as women are usually portrayed in movies as having an orgasm every time they have penetrative sex. The reality, however, is that the majority of women cannot orgasm without clitoral stimulation. If you can orgasm through vaginal penetration without clitoral stimulation, you actually fall within the minority of women. The clitoris is the center of women's pleasure, and so it is imperative for a woman to explore her clitoris and vulva to understand what is pleasurable for her and what helps her achieve orgasm. She can then incorporate her knowledge and understanding of her pleasure into her sexual relationship with her partner. Some of the things couples do to help the woman orgasm are: focusing on her pleasure before or after vaginal penetrative sex through manual stimulation or oral sex; finding positions that stimulate her clitoris (the woman on top is a popular one); manually stimulating her clitoris during PIV sex (either herself, her partner, or with the use of sex toys); and, of course, not even having vaginal intercourse but simply enjoying all forms of sex.

Though the orgasm can be a very pleasurable and important part of sex for many, it is not always necessary as one can achieve pleasure, eroticism, and intimacy without it. In fact, many of these experiences can be enhanced when the orgasm becomes less of a focus. Having an agenda during sex to achieve orgasm can tune a person out of the connection with his/her partner and distract from other meaningful parts of the experience. In addition, focusing on reaching orgasm can create performance anxiety as the client or her partner can get concerned about whether or not it is going to work, how long it is taking, and why she might not be having an orgasm, as opposed to feeling connected to each other and deeply enjoying other erotic and sensual parts of sex that might not necessarily involve stimulating the genitals.

I think it is important to clarify that arousal, pleasure, and intimacy can be achieved through means of non-genital stimulation such as sensual touching of other areas of the body, gazing deeply into each other's eyes, sharing sexual thoughts and fantasies, dressing provocatively or role-playing, teasing, experimenting with different props, watching or reading erotic material together, and other things. Discussing the variety of non-genital intimate activities couples can engage in can tremendously help them create a healthy and enjoyable sexual connection while maintaining a safe and comfortable space. Rather than completely stopping all forms of sexual and intimate experiences due to fear or pain, they can still enjoy different physical, emotional, and mental parts of each other while reducing the pressure of having PIV sex. The Sensate Focus program described in Chapter 6 can also be helpful in supporting the couple through learning to engage in building intimacy through non-genital touch.

Good Sex Means Both Partners Having an Orgasm, Preferably at the Same Time

As described previously, sex is not just about the orgasm. If that were the case, not only would that put too much pressure on performance and on the outcome, but it would also prevent the client from enjoying so many more aspects of sex. Sensuality, connection, fun, spontaneity, romance, anticipation, among other things, are some of the things that make sex an enjoyable and exciting experience. Orgasms often become more difficult to achieve if one focuses too much on them anyway.

In many movies, the couple is portrayed to climax at the same time. And while this is possible, and, for many of us, romantic, it is not the reality for most couples. Sometimes the woman reaches orgasm before, and sometimes the man reaches orgasm and the woman doesn't. Sometimes he continues to pleasure her after vaginal penetrative sex to help her climax, and sometimes not. Sometimes neither reaches orgasm, and that is also fine. I do encourage couples to focus more on touching, petting, and expressing physical affection often, without the expectation of it always leading to vaginal intercourse or orgasm.

If a Woman Shows Interest in Sex, She Must Be Promiscuous or Dirty

Sex is not just for the man's pleasure, and both have the right to enjoy it. A woman enjoying sex has nothing to do with her promiscuity or morals. Believing that a woman enjoying sex means that she is promiscuous simply creates a lot of shame, guilt, and anxiety associated with sex. Reinforcing the idea that a woman should not show interest in sex or enjoy it leads to sex becoming an obligation for her, thus resulting in less interest, less pleasure, and of course potentially more pain and avoidance. It is a natural desire and right for both genders to be interested in sex and to enjoy it. A woman's body is her own, and she has the right to choose what to do with it and how to express her sexuality, and she can still do that in an appropriate manner that is not causing harm to anyone else or to herself. The irony is that many women receive the message that, on the one hand, "respectable" women should not be sexual, and yet, on the other, men want to marry those women and expect them to be interested in having sex with them and to enjoy it. Additionally, a woman's pleasure is just as important as a man's pleasure, and yet many women who do not enjoy sex or do not orgasm do not seek help for that or communicate it with their partner because the belief is that sex is mainly for the man's pleasure.

For women who come from a religious background where they believe that sexual pleasure or interest is "impure," it may be helpful to seek out more accurate information and clarify exactly what her religion truly says about that. Often there is a misconception that religion deems that sex should only be for the purpose of procreation, and therefore that pleasure or desire is secondary, if necessary at all. However, in reality, certain religions such as Islam state that the wife has as much right to have her sexual needs fulfilled as the husband has, and that the husband must also fulfill the wife's sexual needs. I believe that the internal conflict occurs not only due to this potential misconception, but also because of the contradictory messages people receive around sex – that sex is shameful and dirty, and yet you are supposed to enjoy it and have it frequently and easily in your marriage.

Sex Is a Condition for Receiving Love

This myth or belief could be one of the reasons many women engage in sex out of duty or obligation. One of their fears is that if they do not "give" their husbands enough sex, or if their husbands are not sexually satisfied, they might stop loving them, cheat on them, or leave them. Sex is, in this case, used as a means to control the other person, where love is withheld because of the lack of sex. Though this belief and fear are quite common, and sometimes the partner does respond to the woman's lack of sexual desire or engagement with resentment and passive aggressive behavior, it is imperative to work with the couple on shifting this dynamic in the relationship so that sex is not associated with fear or control, but rather with safety and love.

Associating sex with fear or control reflects a sexual abuse mindset. Even if the husband is unaware of his behaviors or reactions, or does not intend to create this type of negative environment, it would be helpful to shed some light on how his responses to his wife's difficulties unintentionally contribute to and potentially exacerbate the fear and avoidance cycle. It is also important to work with the woman on challenging some of her beliefs about her husband withholding love because of sex as she may also be misinterpreting his behaviors in a way that may fit into her unrealistic and negative beliefs about men and sex. It is possible that the husband is avoiding expressing love or affection due to feeling rejected or even to the fear of unintentionally putting pressure on his wife as she may misinterpret his actions as him initiating intimacy.

Sex Is "Doing to" Someone

I often pay very close attention to the language people use to express their thoughts, and I feel this is particularly important when it comes to sex. We sometimes are not aware of our deeply held beliefs and how they influence us, yet our language may reflect them. Statements like "I would do her," "I was doing it to her," though maybe innocently and widely used, could indicate subtle views that sex is something that a man "does" to a woman. This attitude perpetuates the notions that sex is about control, that men enjoy it more than women, that it is for the man's pleasure, and that women are submissive and are the receivers rather than equal participants. This is more aligned with a sexual abuse mindset, where sex feels exploitative, unsafe, hurtful, and transactional, rather than a healthy sexual attitude that fosters feelings of safety, respect, and empowerment.

Hence, I believe it would be useful to check the client's language (and the husband's, if possible) to notice whether or not they believe sex is something that is "done" to them. This is not to say that sex should never be this way – many people do enjoy "being done to" or "doing" at times. At the same time, when the client's (and her partner's) views of sex generally tend to represent a potentially abusive or controlling dynamic when there is already an underlying fear of sex, then I feel it is important to work with her and her husband on not only changing those beliefs to ones that reflect that sex is an *experience* and an expression of self, but on also adapting their sexual behaviors accordingly in order to create a sexual relationship that is mutually respectful. I think one of the key elements that differentiates between an abusive versus a respectful dynamic is *consent*. Consent is not just about giving someone permission, it is the agreement between two parties. I found Betty Martin's Wheel of Consent® to be a super helpful and clear way to depict the different ways to give and receive in a consensual manner. I highly recommend watching her video to gain more insight into this subject (https://youtu.be/auokDp_EA80). To learn more about this topic and her work, visit her websites: www.bettymartin.org and www.schoolofconsent.org.

Shame and Disgust

As I explore some of the misconceptions and negative thoughts around sex that the client may have, I would also want to get a better sense of the client's emotional responses and attitudes toward her own sexuality. From my observations with my clients, it is not uncommon for them to hold a lot of shame around sex, and to at times even be disgusted by the genitals. I find that it makes sense for them to feel shameful around sex considering some of the negative messages they may have learned or formed about it growing up, and that some of them may have even been exposed to uncomfortable or abusive situations.

Shame

As mentioned in the contributing factors, shame and guilt associated with sex during our upbringing can be linked to vaginismus and other sexual difficulties. With clients, it is crucial to think back and reflect on the types of (direct and indirect) messages they received about sex growing up. Direct messages involve clear statements or information they may have received from their family members, peers, school, religious gatherings or readings, magazines, books, the internet, or anyone in their life. Common direct messages come from sex education at school (if it was provided), or people directly expressing their opinions or information they have. For example, a parent telling their daughter: "Sex before marriage is wrong" is a direct message.

Indirect messages, however, are more subtle, are more difficult to remember or recognize, and in my opinion, are much more commonly shared, and could even sometimes be more impactful (positively or negatively). Indirect messages involve judgments, facial expressions, body language, and behaviors that could create negative or positive associations. For example, hearing your neighbor gossip about another neighbor's dating life is an indirect message that could contribute to your belief system about what is acceptable or unacceptable for women to do. Even the lack of communication about sex in the family is an indirect message that could create shame around it. Below are some questions to bring up with a client to assess her attitudes around sex and gain a deeper understanding of what kinds of messages she may have indirectly received about sex growing up.

Sexual Attitudes and Indirect Messages About Sex Worksheet

Was sex a topic that could be openly discussed at home?

How did the parents react if the child showed any curiosity about their genitals or sex? For example, did they punish them, reassure them, or shame them?

How did the parents respond when anything sexual came up on TV? For example, did they immediately change channels, show disgust and shame, or ask the child to leave the room or close their eyes?

How physically affectionate or distant were the parents with each other?

Did anyone ever talk to them about sex, and if yes, what did they say?

Were other people judged or shamed because of their romantic or sexual interests or experience?

Were boys encouraged to explore their sexualities while girls were expected to stay "pure"?

Were women shamed for being in relationships before marriage?

Did the clients feel safe being interested in boys or relationships or were they afraid of how their parents might react if they found out?

Were women encouraged or discouraged to dress in certain ways? What was considered appropriate and inappropriate?

What is the client's earliest sexual memory? This could be a sexual experience she engaged in or an event she witnessed or learned about.

When did the client first become aware of the opposite sex? How did the client feel about that at the time?

What did the client learn or know about childbirth and contraception?

How did the client's parents/family feel about nudity around the house?

How much privacy did the client have as a child and adolescent?

Was religion observed in the family growing up? How did that affect the client's attitudes toward sex?

How does the client's religious beliefs currently affect her feelings about sex?

Was there any infidelity in the family growing up, and if yes, how did that influence the client's views on sex, relationships, and trust?

It is very common for the clients to have not had any clear or direct conversations with their parents about sex growing up. Nonetheless, as children we pick up on subtle things such as our parents' body language and things they say (or don't say) when anything related to sex or romantic relationships comes up. These moments get ingrained in our unconscious as either negative or positive associations, leading to us feeling either safe and relaxed about sex, ashamed and anxious about it, or confused and conflicted. When the client does not remember specific events, it could be helpful to pay attention to how she feels about sexual conversations and situations. I would encourage the client to notice how she feels about other people's and women's sexual experiences, and to tune into any bodily sensations or emotions she may be experiencing as we discuss certain sexual topics or beliefs. If the client tends to judge others or have negative emotions associated with sex, then she most likely grew up in an environment (either at home or in her society) that discouraged or shamed it.

If that is the case, then it is time for us to work on her questioning her feelings:

> How does she truly feel about sex, and why?
> What are the first words or beliefs that come up when the word "sex" is mentioned?
> Does she think it is shameful?
> What types of sexual activities or experiences are shameful, and which are acceptable?
> Does she think women who enjoy it are bad?
> Does she think it is wrong to know her body and feel good about it?
> How does she feel about her body? Her breasts? Her vulva?
> How does she feel about men? What statements or beliefs does she hold about men? For example, "Men only want sex," or "All men care about is sex."

These are just some of the questions one can explore during this process to shed some light on her sexual attitudes. In order to challenge and potentially change some of the negative and dysfunctional beliefs about sex, it can be helpful to also think about where the client gets those beliefs from, and most of the time she will realize that she just has them but never really thought about them. It might be time to open her mind and change her view about some of her judgments.

Case Example

> One of my courageous clients, Najwa, who was from Egypt, shared with me that not only did no one in her family talk to her about menstruation or sex, but she also heard her parents talk negatively about other girls and women whom they judged as sexual. She also remembered being shamed about her genitals and her sexual feelings as a young adolescent – as if it was bad or wrong to get these uncontrollable sensations in her genital area as she began her sexual development. At that young age she did not understand what those feelings were, but she remembers knowing that it was not right to acknowledge those sensations and urges, let alone explore them in any way. She also did not feel comfortable to ask questions or express her concerns about her sensations because she knew she would be shut down and judged. Those subtle messages Najwa received as a teen about genitals and sexual feelings are quite common. One can see how these experiences can contribute to her feeling uncomfortable with and ashamed of her genitals and of sexual sensations and feelings.

Disgust

In addition to the fear of pain or penetration being one of the leading factors behind unconsummated marriages in Arab cultures (Muammar et al., 2015), disgust around the female and male genitals and fluids is another factor that contributes to GPPPD, vaginal penetration phobia, or general resistance or anxiety around sex. Though some of the clients who have disgust around the genitals tend to be squeamish around other bodily functions, I have found that disgust is often associated with the shame clients hold around sex. If a person is taught or told (directly or indirectly) that sex is dirty, shameful, and taboo, then it likely becomes associated with a deep feeling of disgust that can even sometimes create a visceral response. Dirty equals disgusting. In addition, there is often negative messaging around menstruation being unhygienic, and that the woman is dirty or "impure" when she is menstruating. This could also contribute to a feeling of disgust and shame around the female genitals.

When a client expresses or indicates disgust around her genitals, I usually spend additional time working on reframing her view of her vulva to a more neutral, and, if possible, positive one. I often explore times in their lives where they were able to (consciously or subconsciously) shift their views of other objects from "disgusting" to neutral or enjoyable. Examples of that are types of foods that the person may have, at one point in her life, been repulsed by, and then at a different stage in her life changed her view of and learned to enjoy. Brussel sprouts are one example! Consequently, it would be useful to learn from these types of experiences about what helps the client shift her feelings and beliefs about something, and experiment with mental exercises to practice that with her genitals.

As we know in therapy, simply discussing a topic and mentally shifting one's view of things is not always sufficient to create a significant change, and so being able to practice having a different experience also helps reframe one's feelings and beliefs on a more fundamental level. This can be achieved through some of the practical Solo Exercises around exploring her body in Chapter 5. One way to create new mental connections through dialogue is to discuss what the vulva or female genitals represent to the client. Words such as "disgusting" or "dirty" or "period" may come up. In order to create more positive associations with her vulva, I would explore other meanings or themes that are also attached to the female genitals such as "pleasure," "intimacy," "giving life," and "expression of love and connection." The mouth is a part of our body that produces fluids and is involved in basic activities such as eating and drinking, which could be deemed "disgusting," and yet it is also used as a means to express love, affection, and desire through kissing, licking, and sucking. In a similar fashion then this can be used as an example of how we can reframe the vulva to encompass many different things and not be disgusting.

Following the train of thought that some objects or experiences could feel "disgusting" in some situations while in other situations they could feel neutral or even enjoyable, I sometimes describe certain analogies to clients to help create new mental connections around sex. For example, many of us would feel disgusted sharing a cup of water or taking a bite off of a sandwich with a stranger, or even an acquaintance. On the other hand, when it comes to a loved one, we are more than happy to share food, drinks, and even exchange fluids with them through kissing and other sexual acts. Think about how mothers generally do not feel disgusted by their babies' saliva or even excrement, simply because the care and love of a mother overpowers the disgust. Nonetheless, that same mother might feel more disgusted about someone else's saliva or poop. Similarly, though viewing genitals may feel disgusting at times, the client may feel differently about the genitals of the person she loves and is attracted to. Along those lines, if she is able to achieve a more positive and loving view of herself as well, one would expect her to feel more neutral or even positive about her genitals.

Interestingly, it has been shown that when women were sexually aroused, they rated the sex-relevant disgusting stimuli as less disgusting and were more willing to approach disgusting stimuli, thus reducing disgust-avoidance behaviors. This suggests that high sexual arousal could not only shift the person's perspective of what they find disgusting, but could also encourage them or facilitate their openness to engage in them because the arousal overpowers the disgust (Borg & Jong, 2012). Therefore, when looking at GPPPD, it seems highly important to factor in how sexually aroused the client is, and that if she is not sufficiently excited or aroused this may contribute to the maintenance of penetration difficulties. Building on this finding, if the client does theoretically feel disgusted about sex or certain sexual acts, she may be able to shift her perspective of these sexual experiences with her loved one to a more positive one and be more interested in engaging in pleasurable sexual activities if the couple is supported through creating sufficient arousal and pleasure. Having or creating sufficient sexual arousal within the realms of traditional or arranged marriages can sometimes prove to be a challenging goal, as the marriage is often not based on initial attraction or connection. For this reason, I usually pay quite a bit of attention in these specific cases to strengthening the inter-personal relationship between the couple, in order for the woman to build the trust and connection with her husband that could lead to the development of desire and arousal. This is a big part of why I tend to tackle penetration difficulties from a more integrated way rather than just focusing on the practical and pelvic exercises. Sensate Focus (described in Chapter 6) is one method that can help the couple create arousal.

Another mental and practical exercise I often explore with clients who feel disgust around their genitals is to encourage them to visualize their vulvas as different types of flowers or roses blooming. They could also draw or illustrate different flowers they view as beautiful into a picture of a vulva to help reinforce that image in their minds. In this modern day of social media and the internet, I have come across several accounts of artists who illustrate or paint different images, perspectives, and expressive versions of the female body, the genitals, sex, and intimacy. I would encourage the clients to seek out different sex positive resources to normalize the genitals and sex like those (@womeninspireart and @vielma.at and @the.vulva.gallery on Instagram). Figure 2.2 is an example of a wonderful image of a blossoming vulva.

Figure 2.2 Vulva flower.

Trauma and Sexual Abuse

Before going into how sexual trauma could impact a woman's sexuality, I would like to note that the majority of the women who presented to me with GPPPD during my years practicing in the UAE did not report a history of sexual abuse. It could be the case that some of these women either do not remember the abuse or did not want to disclose it out of fear or shame, especially considering the traditional and conservative culture they come from. And so while sexual trauma did not necessarily take a very large chunk of my work with most of my female clients with GPPPD, it does not mean that it does not exist and is not prominent. I believe, therefore, that it is an important topic to assess and work through as it could significantly impact a person's sexual feelings and behaviors.

Evidence for the role of childhood sexual abuse or sexual trauma in the development of vaginismus has been mixed. Though in one study it was found that women in the vaginismus group were more than twice as likely to have a history of sexual interference in childhood (Reissing et al., 2003), no link between childhood abuse and vaginismus was found in others (Tetik et al., 2020). Despite the mixed results, I find that it is still important in the process of therapy for any client, especially those struggling with intimacy or sexual issues, to assess for and address any history of sexual abuse. Sexual abuse could constitute rape, though in the majority of the cases the abuse is more subtle and involves other sexually inappropriate behaviors such as molestation, oral copulation, exposing of genitals, and masturbating in front of the person/child. While the perpetrators could be strangers, they are more often than not close to the person such as immediate or extended family members or other people in the community. When we hear sexual abuse, we often think of violent acts of rape committed by strangers stalking us in a dark alley at night. And while this does happen, most of the time the abuse occurs among people the child knows and trusts, and there tends to be a grooming process where the child is gradually manipulated by the perpetrator into performing or receiving certain acts and not disclosing them to anyone. The perpetrators may even convince the child that these are acts of love, and that telling someone about it would be a betrayal of that love, or that the person finding out about this information would not believe them, or even worse, would punish them for it.

When assessing whether or not sexual abuse has occurred, I feel it is important to firstly educate the client on these facts as most clients might also assume that only violent and extreme cases of sexual assault count. Therefore, enlightening the client on how sexual abuse could be more subtle and learning to trust that if the client remembers any event that may have felt unsafe or uncomfortable sexually it could be an indication of sexual abuse that requires further exploration, may be part of the assessment process. For example, a client may have never been inappropriately touched by anyone, but may have had an older cousin expose himself to her without her permission (and even if she consented to it, she may have been too young to understand what that means, hence negating the consent). A different example could be a male family member playing with the child on his lap, getting erect, and continuing to play.

Though these events may not register in the child's mind as abuse (people tend to recognize later in life anyway that certain events were abusive), they most likely will have an effect; whether it is just an uncomfortable feeling, or confusion, or some shame, or even guilt. Additionally, the child may experience some curiosity or arousal during the abuse as a natural physiological response, which at a later stage in adulthood may create even more shame and disgust thinking they "enjoyed" the experience. Another common experience that leads to guilt is when the client blames him/herself for not saying no or not leaving the situation at the time. When they look back at the situation later in life, they feel guilty and ashamed of the fact that they did not stand up for themselves, defend themselves, tell anyone, or end the abuse. Part of the work therefore may need to include getting the client to a place where they trust that they did everything they could in that moment to protect themselves, to realize that the abuse was not their fault, but the fault of the perpetrator, and to forgive themselves. They need to remember that they were young, vulnerable, and scared at the time, as opposed to how they may feel as adults looking back at it, and give their younger self the security and comfort they needed then. They may even feel like thanking their younger self for doing the best they could at the time to keep themselves safe.

The effect of sexual abuse on one's feelings about sex and sexual behaviors can be devastating and varies significantly from one survivor to another. Within the context of GPPPD, and considering how impactful shame and trust are for women suffering from penetration difficulties, it is not surprising that sexual abuse can contribute to the shame and fear associated with sex. If some of their early sexual experiences involved non-consensual and most likely scary or intimidating behaviors, that could create a foundation of fear, helplessness, vulnerability, and a lack of trust regarding sex and sexual partners. In addition, having kept the abuse a secret creates even more shame and guilt around sex that might not be spoken about within her relationship, thus potentially leading to some confusion in the client and the partner during sex. Furthermore, this cycle could reinforce the client's difficulty and lack of confidence in speaking up about her needs, feelings, and boundaries, thus putting her in a powerless position where she continues to engage in and potentially be subjected to sexual behaviors that she does not feel comfortable with. Compound the general shame around sex with the secrecy and powerlessness around the sexual abuse the client endured, and you could have someone who would continue to silently bear the discomfort, pain, and emotional trauma sex could be triggering for her. This highlights the importance of working on the client feeling more empowered with her sexuality, her leading the process based on her readiness, and her speaking up in general, in addition to building trust in her relationship.

3 Between Control and Vulnerability

As mentioned earlier, feeling in control is crucial for women to be able to overcome their fears. Being in control helps them feel safe, which in turn enables them to feel more confident to attempt certain things that may feel difficult. Therefore, throughout their treatment process, I would strongly encourage them to go through the solo and partner exercises described in later chapters at their own pace, and to not take big risks they are not ready for just because they feel pressured to do so. Gaining a sense of control also happens through learning to be assertive, authentic, and relaxed in other parts of one's life as well, and becoming a more integrated person, which is what this chapter focuses on.

The Purpose of Vaginismus

In my practice with clients, I look at their whole lives in the process of the therapy as I often see many parallels in how they approach other things in life. For example, I noticed that many women who worked with me and experienced vaginismus or vaginal penetration phobia tended to be quite anxious (as mentioned in Chapter 1), and may even be considered or judged as rigid at times. This could indicate that they generally do not feel they have much control over certain areas in life, and try to exert control where they could. If they are in a situation they fear or worry about and do not feel in control of, they may struggle. Sex could be one of the few areas where control could be imposed or manifested, and vaginismus may be serving a positive function for them in this case. One way I like to look at sexual dysfunctions (and other relationship or personal "problems" for that matter) is to ask how that problem is serving the person. I tend to avoid labeling the clients' difficulties as "problems" or "dysfunctions" because I generally view them as logical and purposeful (Bancroft, Loftus, & Long, 2003). There is often a (subconscious) purpose the behavior is serving, and I find that it is usually to protect the client. What is the vaginismus doing for the client? And one of my favorite questions is to ask the client: "If your body could speak, what would it be saying?" Some of the answers to that question that I've heard, among others, are: "I don't want this," "I'm scared," "I don't trust you," "I don't want to lose control," or "I'm not ready."

DOI: 10.4324/9781003129172-3

In one study on the sufferers' self-perceptions, one woman suffering from vaginismus quoted the following: "I do feel very strongly that for me personally vaginismus is part of a much bigger problem about how I feel about myself and build a protective shell around myself, and cannot be treated as a separate sexual dysfunction" (Ward & Ogden, 1994).

The body shares a lot of wisdom, and we just need to learn to listen better. Understanding what the client's body is trying to do for her can help us support her through creating the mental, physical, and emotional environment that she needs in order to feel safe and confident. Therefore, if she has a deeper fear that her body is trying to protect her from, working through her fears cognitively, behaviorally, and relationally will eventually help her body learn to relax and let go of needing to control the situation. Another example of how vaginismus may be serving as a defense mechanism is what one of the women suffering from vaginismus expressed regarding her beliefs:

> I believe I developed vaginismus at a very young age as a defense to a controlling mother who wouldn't allow me to "separate" into another human being. I put a false physical barrier around myself to provide a safe retreat, safe from invasion, and to prevent merger with her, i.e. disintegration of self.
>
> (Ward & Ogden, 1994)

Another way I sometimes explore how the dysfunction is serving the client is by playing with metaphors. For example, we could look at what the vaginismus represents metaphorically speaking in the client's life. Similarly, one could ask what metaphors exist around sex, or the vagina, or the penis. Themes like sex representing "losing oneself," and the vaginismus being a metaphor for boundaries or protection can provide us with deep insight into how the client feels about intimacy and relationships. If there is a fear of being "consumed" or "intruded upon," then it is highly likely that the client never learned how to set healthy boundaries and differentiate from others. Letting someone in and being vulnerable, exposed, and seen, can be very scary when the client's experience of those relationships has been painful, intense, dismissive, or abusive. There may also be a fear of losing others, and so while the client may be afraid of allowing people in, she might also be fearful of being abandoned if they get too close and do not love what they see. If the vagina is viewed as "ugly" or "disgusting," could this be a metaphor for how the client truly feels about herself deep down? Similarly with the male organs – if the penis is viewed as "threatening" or "dangerous," might we be really talking about the client's perception or experience of men as such? Does "sex" then reflect intimacy and relationships being vulnerable, scary, and painful?

Exploring the deeper meanings underneath the vaginismus can help us support the client through creating a more loving relationship with herself, a more trusting view of others, and a wholesome sense of self. The idea is that when she becomes a more whole and differentiated individual with healthy boundaries and connections, she will not need to exert such control when it comes to sex. Control, within the realm of penetration difficulties, is clearly a significant theme, and so part of my work with clients is to help them learn how to establish a healthy and functional balance between maintaining their sense of control and letting go of it.

Generally speaking, it is a natural response to avoid situations we do not feel safe in or that lead to negative feelings, but problems arise when avoiding sex starts to cause significant distress to the person and negatively impacts the relationship. Assuming that feeling more in control of our feelings and lives leads to feeling safer, it therefore makes sense to empower these women so that they feel more in control and less fearful. This is why it is very important for them to be leading this process at a pace that they feel comfortable with. "Comfortable" should not be confused with "avoidance," however, as overcoming challenges does not happen without some discomfort or anxiety. One way to look at what pace would work for the client is that it should stretch them a little but not break them. There should be some discomfort that they feel confident in being able to deal with, but not too much anxiety or discomfort that they do not feel safe. Therefore, when the client is attempting some of the mental or practical exercises, it is natural for her to feel anxious or uncomfortable, but the level of discomfort should be bearable so that she is able to deal with it temporarily until it subsides and she is able to move forward.

In addition to being in control of how they work through the exercises, I encourage the clients to look at their relationship and life in general, and think of areas they need to feel more empowered in, while at the same time reflecting on areas they think they need to learn to be more relaxed in. For example, do they speak up about their needs and feelings often? Do they set enough healthy boundaries with people, or do they feel intruded/invaded upon often? Do they allow themselves to express themselves, or do they hold back? In my discussions with clients, I would support them in reflecting on their relationship with their partner and friends/family and think about whether they often feel they are not getting their needs met or their feelings heard. We would also explore whether they are clearly explaining what they need and expressing what is OK and not OK for them. Often, they find that the answer is no, and that what they need to do is learn to be more assertive.

Assertiveness

Assertiveness is a very common skill I end up working on with most clients, regardless of the presenting issue, as it is one that many people often lack. We were never taught how to do it, and we certainly are not born with that ability, but the good news is that it is something we can learn and become more skilled at. There is a wonderful book for women by Anne Dickson called *A Woman in Your Own Right* that very clearly explains what assertiveness means and how to practice it as a woman. I believe it is even more important to work on empowering clients, especially women, in my part of the world because it is generally not encouraged for people to speak up as it may be considered "rude" or "selfish" in such cultures. The concern around not upsetting or disrespecting others, for example relatives or people who are older, tends to be high in Middle-Eastern cultures and we often grow up learning that expressing ourselves is shameful, especially if it may come across as "rude." Even refusing offers, such as offering food, can be quite tough as people tend to have difficulty taking "no" for an answer. Setting boundaries and standing their ground can be really challenging in a situation like this. It seems quite clear to me then that when we learn that our needs, desires, or even boundaries are selfish or rude, we are less likely to speak up as adults, and therefore have less power and feel less safe.

This section of the book will provide some tips on how to help clients enhance their ability to assert themselves. It is important to keep the cultural nuances in mind and be tactful in how the client speaks up for herself, especially as she is starting to build that skill, so that we do not completely alienate her from her society. Of course, there are certain "risks" that may come with speaking up, such as others feeling disappointed or upset, or certain relationships changing, but these risks can be diminished or mitigated if it is practiced in a skillful and culturally sensitive way. Just as being assertive comes with risks, not speaking up comes with the risks of not getting her needs met, not being able to protect herself from potential emotional, psychological, or physical abuse, not getting what is rightfully hers, and building resentment, among other things. Therefore, one of the ways I take culture into consideration and work sensitively with my clients is to guide her through evaluating what types of risks she is willing to take in each situation, and what benefits and negative consequences she might get. That way, she can make conscious choices regarding when and where she wants to be more assertive. For example, if asserting herself with a distant relative might result in significant criticism and backlash from her parents, and she would rather tolerate this relative's behaviors on an occasional basis instead, then this might be a situation where she chooses not to assert herself.

During my sessions with my clients, I would explore and discuss with them some of the questions below to assess how easy they find it to assert themselves. Usually, the way I would assess is by having a fluid conversation with the client about these questions and points, not through a structured or formal questionnaire. I have laid out some of the main questions that could help guide the clinician evaluate the client's assertiveness skills below, and I would encourage the clinician to use her/his judgment and experience to modify and add to these questions depending on the situation.

Assertiveness Assessment Guidelines

How difficult do you find it to say no to things you do not want to do? That could range from anything like not wanting to have Chinese food for dinner, to not wanting to have sex. With whom do you find it most difficult and easiest to do so?

How difficult do you find it to tell the person when something hurts you, upsets you, or makes you feel uncomfortable? That could be when someone says something directly hurtful to you, or when your boss treats you in a less professional manner.

How much do you tend to please people? When people ask you for favors or requests, how often do you go out of your way to make them happy? How frequently does this lead to you letting go of things you wanted to do or changing plans, or even causing you frustration or distress?

How often do you feel you are not being appreciated enough? Like you do so much for others, but it is not reciprocated, or it is taken for granted?

How easy is it for you to ask for things you want? How about making requests from people who are close to you, and people you are less comfortable with? And when you do, how difficult does it feel?

How strong is your belief that you deserve to be treated with respect and have the right to say no or ask for what you want? How much more concerned are you about causing others inconvenience compared to getting what is rightfully yours?

If the client mostly finds it difficult to ask for what is rightfully hers, to set boundaries, to express her needs, and ends up being more concerned about not disappointing others, then these responses suggest that asserting herself is challenging for her. When people have trouble being assertive, that could lead to resentment in their relationships and a build-up of frustrations and feeling unappreciated. It also undermines their power in relationships, which is why I believe it is very important for a client's own sense of empowerment to strengthen this skill.

<u>Assertiveness Training Worksheet</u>

One of the ways I often suggest to start learning this skill is to first make a list of ten situations you find difficult saying "no" to, in increasing order of difficulty (1 being the least difficult, and 10 being the most difficult). Next, I would suggest you start practicing saying no to situations that are similar to number 1 until you build more confidence to move on to situations like number 2, and then number 3, etc. It is important for you to only move on to the more challenging ones after you have mastered the easier ones and have built more confidence.

There is an art to saying "no," and so if she is afraid of being rude or upsetting people, here are some tips I usually suggest to the client on how to relay the message in a kind and firm way:

1- <u>Use "I" language</u>. *Start sentences with "I" rather than "you" to avoid unintentionally blaming or accusing people. It is very common for people to say* things like "you shouldn't have ..." or "you never listen" or "you always do this," which immediately puts the other person in a defensive mode, hence making it difficult for them to listen and have a constructive conversation. The discussion is instantly set up for an argument or a path of pointing fingers and judging who is right or wrong. Instead, saying things like "I don't feel comfortable doing this" or "I would rather not go there" or "I am not available at that time" reduces the likelihood of the listener feeling blamed. In addition, saying "I" empowers you as you take responsibility for things and start nurturing the belief that <u>you have the right to say no</u>.

Furthermore, though you may be inclined to give an explanation that you feel is "good enough" to refuse a request, I invite you to try to simply say you do not want to do something or are not comfortable with something without overly justifying it. You have the right to say no, and your reason does not have to be valid enough for others. Sometimes we do not want to do something because we just want to relax or have other desires, and we often feel guilty that our reasons are not valid, so we compromise our own needs to make others happy. I encourage you to internally give yourself permission to prioritize your needs from time to time.

2- <u>Tone is (almost) everything.</u> Most of the time it is not what we say, but it is how we say things that make the biggest impact. You can say the exact same sentence in two different tones of voice, and they will have a completely different impact on the listener. Make sure your tone is kind, calm, clear, and confident – avoid sarcastic, passive aggressive, or aggressive comments.

3- <u>Be firm and specific.</u> Setting clear boundaries is extremely important in order for you to set the tone and encourage people to respect your boundaries in the future. Be specific about what it is you do not like or do not want to do, and what you do like and want, and avoid general and vague statements. For example, saying something like "I really don't want Chinese food" is clear and firm, as opposed to "Umm I'd rather not, but if you want, that's OK, we can go for Chinese food." The second statement implies that you are OK with Chinese food, whereas if you really do not like it, the first statement is more congruent to how you feel.

If you go along with the second type of statement often, people are more likely to ask you to go for Chinese food again in the future because they do not know how much you dislike it, which will continue to frustrate you. Whereas if you are firmer and clear, as in the first example, they are less likely to push for Chinese food in the future. You may need to repeat it once or twice again in the future, people do not necessarily remember and change instantly, but you will most likely need to repeat it less frequently and the outcome will tend to be more successful with more clarity. You can still be kind while being firm. For example, saying something like: "I really want to see you and spend time with you, but I don't like Chinese food. How about we go to that Italian place instead?"

4- <u>Make a request for change.</u> When we refuse something, it is a good idea to suggest something else instead. This helps the receiver know what to do instead in the future and gives you both an opportunity to resolve the

Between Control and Vulnerability 47

disagreement in the moment. Therefore, after you have clearly stated that you do not want Chinese food, make another suggestion of a type of food you like. (Apologies for picking on Chinese food as a random example, I do not have anything against it, in fact, I am quite a fan!).

5- <u>Stick to what you said.</u> It is important to recognize that simply being more assertive verbally is not always enough for people to respect your boundaries and fulfill your needs. People might sometimes still act in ways that contradict what you expressed, and this could happen more often when you start practicing assertiveness as people are still adapting to the new firm and confident you. Therefore, your actions need to also reflect what you are asking for or refusing. For example, if you clearly express to your spouse that you really do not like Chinese food, then you need to stop ordering Chinese food. If you continue to order and eat Chinese food, then your dislike of it will most likely not be taken as seriously as it really is.

However, if you stand your ground and choose not to order and eat Chinese food, then your spouse will most likely realize how strongly you feel about it. Obviously, there is the chance that he will still want Chinese food, and this is where you can both negotiate another solution together (for example, you can pick up Chinese food for him and Italian food for you). Otherwise, you can choose to let this go and accept eating Chinese food once in a while if it is not highly important to you and you would like to give your partner that joy. The example of types of cuisine is a relatively simple one here, and of course in life and relationships it is possible that you will disagree on a subject that is extremely important for both of you, which can continue to create conflict. If after negotiating solutions you are still unable to find a middle ground, then I would encourage you to seek professional help from a couples therapist. The point here, however, is that there are several potential outcomes to you setting a boundary, and we cannot control how other people will respond, but the more aligned your actions are to your words, the more likely people are to take your needs seriously.

6- <u>Accept that it may upset others.</u> Following the previous line of thinking, though you are in control of what you say, how you say it, and what you do, you are not in control of how others will feel about it or respond to it. Setting boundaries comes with the risk of potentially upsetting or disappointing others, even though that may not be your intention or desired outcome. It is up to you to choose when you are willing to "risk" disappointing others, when your needs are more important, and when you are willing to let go of some of your needs and desires because making someone else happy is more valuable in that particular situation. As you may notice, I am not suggesting that saying no is always right, or that accommodating others is always wrong. I am suggesting that our decisions should come from a more conscious place of caring for ourselves and others rather than a place of fearing rejection or disappointment.

After you have mastered the art of saying "no," you can move on to practicing how to make requests and ask for what is rightfully yours. In a similar manner to the above, I would invite you to make a list of ten things you find difficult to ask *for (in order of increasing difficulty), and practice each level over a couple of weeks or so until you feel confident enough to move on to the next level.*

Relating assertiveness to sex, once the client starts building confidence within herself and her relationship in terms of being able to set boundaries and express her needs and desires, she can start implementing this skill in their sexual life. She can even make a list of things she finds difficult refusing or asking for when it comes to sex and practice progressively building assertiveness and confidence similarly to the general approach described earlier. I find that it might be easier for the client to first start practicing assertiveness in general areas of life before implementing it in sexual topics as many people often find sex to be a difficult topic to discuss to begin with, which might be a more challenging area to practice this new skill in.

Authenticity

Becoming more assertive helps the woman in her journey of building confidence and feeling more empowered, which then helps her feel more in control in her life. In addition to assertiveness, leading a more authentic life supports a person in feeling more in control and relaxed. Therefore, another area I explore with clients is around making more conscious and congruent choices in life. When our actions are not aligned with our values and who we are, we feel anxious and lost – states that do not promote a feeling of being in control or confidence.

For example, if honesty is important to her, and she is not being honest in a certain situation (or many), she will most likely feel anxiety (sometimes camouflaged by guilt). And anxiety usually does not help us feel in control. When she is honest, on the other hand, she is more likely to feel more relaxed and confident, even though it may be difficult to express herself honestly. It is a similar concept to assertiveness where doing things we are genuinely willing to do will empower us more than doing things we unwillingly tolerate. Consequently, behaving in ways and making choices that are congruent with our values contribute to our wellbeing and sense of control.

Living a congruent life is another way of describing authenticity. When the client is authentic, she is her true self – meaning she is clear and genuine with who she is, what she feels, what she wants, and what she does. She does not pretend to be something she is not, or act in ways that are not true to who she is. This sounds very black and white and perfect, so we must acknowledge the reality that we all sometimes live less authentically, and there is a lot of gray in between. But the closer we are to our authentic self, the more at peace and empowered we will be.

Through this part of my work with the client, we would explore how authentic she is with her partner, friends, family, and people in general. I would guide her through reflecting on the values that are important to her in life, ranging from the most important to the least important one, and then discuss where her actions do not align with her values and where they do align. We would also explore how not aligning her behaviors to her values impacts her emotions and thoughts and consequent responses. It could also be helpful to evaluate the values she believes in within specific areas of her life (for example, her values around relationships, her health, her career, her social life, etc.), and to then think about how much she truly follows them. If we find that her actions are often not congruent to her values, and that is causing her distress, then we might start taking steps in therapy toward her changing either how she views that particular issue, or her behavior accordingly, especially with the most important values.

When looking at the client's values, I would explore where those beliefs came from; are they things she has consciously chosen, or rules based on what she thinks she "should" be doing? "Should" is a word I frequently hear in my practice. I am even guilty myself of using that word too often to tell myself how to live my life. I pay a lot of attention to the client's language and often pick up on the excessive use of that word. The reason I believe this word is significant is because it is often representative of the beliefs and expectations we have adopted from our culture/family/society as opposed to what we consciously believe in. Therefore, when we constantly assess our life according to the scripts of others, it can create a performance-based mindset, as opposed to living a life that is congruent to our authentic self. My view is that when we make choices based on what we think we "should" be doing, we become more self-critical, and it becomes more difficult to know what standard is "good enough" for others. And when we do not act according to those rules, we can more easily get consumed with anxiety and/or guilt.

This is why I would be inclined to reinforce more compassion and tenderness toward the self in our work. I would support the client through firstly noticing when her internal dialogue is self-critical and negative, and secondly adopting a more empathetic and compassionate approach toward herself instead. One approach I use is to suggest that the client converses with herself internally as if she was speaking to a loved one or a child. If a child or loved one made a mistake or was not "perfect," she would most likely be more tender and understanding with them. Therefore, she can use that framework to learn how to validate her feelings and acknowledge her struggles, while being compassionate with herself rather than beating herself up about not having done something or performed up to a certain standard. Being kind and compassionate toward the self does not mean letting go of all responsibility. Just like with a child or loved one, when they are struggling, we can find a way to support them through taking ownership and overcoming their challenges with kindness rather than harshness or judgment.

If I notice that "should" is a major part of the client's narrative, I encourage the client to replace the word "should" with "want," so that she can experience how it feels to connect with what she desires rather than what she is expected to do. Changing the language can be quite powerful to some clients, and when they say "want," it firstly gives them the chance to tap into how it feels when they use that word in order to gain insight into whether or not it is aligned with what they truly want. "I *should* spend more time with my family" changes to "I *want* to spend more time with my family," and that can help the client connect with whether or not that statement resonates with her. Secondly, using "want" gives them a sense of ownership over their choices, thus contributing to their sense of empowerment and assertiveness.

I view authenticity as linked to assertiveness. It takes assertiveness to be authentic as you refuse things that do not feel aligned for you, and you choose and request things that do. At the same time, it takes authenticity to be assertive as you need clarity about who you are, what you believe in, and what you want in order for you to ask for that. They feed into and build each other.

Case Example

Mariam is a 28 year-old married woman from Syria who started working with me because vaginal penetrative sex was difficult due to her being tense, anxious, and ashamed. In addition to the self-sensate program she worked through, we frequently discussed how her need to please others was creating so much anxiety and stress, and how practicing assertiveness would help her feel more confident and relaxed. At first, she found that it was really difficult to assert herself, even with friends, as she was afraid of losing some of her friends as a result. She thought that if she started speaking up or saying no to things, then her friends wouldn't like her anymore. This tendency to please others also started to create tremendous stress at work, so that she was becoming unhappy and crying often.

One day, she simply realized that if her friends were not going to like her for who she is, or respect her desires and needs too, that they were not true friends after all. She started to speak up, little by little, and though a couple of her friends were surprised and potentially annoyed by that, other friends commented on how she seemed happier and more relaxed. She is now a more congruent and confident version of herself, and even at work has set more boundaries and shrugged off some of the things she used to take personally. This has also reflected onto her marriage where she has developed the courage to speak up more clearly. Not surprisingly, her husband has appreciated the more empowered and happier woman she has become. Building assertiveness and taking better care of herself has allowed her to show up more authentically in her life and marriage, which tremendously helped them achieve a more positive sexual relationship and connection.

Letting Go

It can sound quite contradictory, but in addition to the client building her sense of control, learning to let go of needing to control things or herself is also an important ability to acquire. This is different than being passive in life or removing her sense of responsibility, but it is more linked to being able to deal with situations where she may not be in as much control as she would like to be, and situations where holding back is negatively impacting her life. As we all know, we cannot control everything in life, and though in the previous section I was encouraging the client to gain a sense of control in her decisions and actions, at the same time I encourage her to learn to let go of control in other situations.

Let me elaborate. Often the need to be in control comes with a tendency to be a perfectionist, which means that the woman sets high standards for herself which are often unrealistic. This can then lead to her being hard on herself (criticizing and putting herself down when she thinks she is not "good enough"). Though it can be admirable to strive for greatness, there is a fine line to when it becomes more harmful and unhealthy. The downfall is that aiming for such unrealistic expectations can lead to disappointment and anxiety (as she worries about not making it), in addition to having high expectations of others (namely her partner), which puts pressure on the relationship and causes more disappointment.

Often there is also a concern about people's judgments, and this is part of the "letting go" process I'm talking about – to reach a place where other people's opinions do not affect her as much. This is usually achieved when her view of herself is not based on the judgment of others but is instead based on her own sense of self. This does not mean that she should not care about other people, or that she is now entitled to cause harm to others, it just means that she can be authentic while still being kind, and that she accepts that she is not going to be liked by everyone. Living our life trying to please everyone is extremely difficult, because it is impossible to be liked by everyone. Therefore, part of learning to let go is accepting that we cannot control what other people feel, think, or do, and being at peace with the fact that there will always be people who will not approve of some of our decisions or behaviors, or will simply not like us.

Case Example

Another one of my clients, Sarah, started to realize more and more throughout our sessions that she often does not know what she really wants because she makes decisions based on pleasing others. This often leads to her feeling anxious about potentially disappointing others, and resentful toward her friends or colleagues for not respecting or valuing her wishes. However, she came to understand that she had not been expressing or asserting her true desires because of a fear of being judged or disliked, and so she never really gave her friends or colleagues the opportunity to take her wishes into consideration. She also acknowledged that by starting to do so, she risks losing some of her friends or changing the nature of some of her relationships as revealing her true self might not be well received by everyone. She came to accept that possibility as she realized that it is more important to her to be genuinely liked for who she is by some, rather than to be liked by others for whom she portrays herself to be. Once she started speaking up

> more, she felt much more empowered and confident, despite having disappointed or surprised some of her friends.

One of the reasons this is important is because it will reduce the client's performance anxiety and self-consciousness. Part of the issue with vaginismus or other sexual difficulties in women is that they are often very worried about people's judgments, mainly their partner's. They often worry if they are attractive enough, or good enough in bed, or if sex will be as great as they think it should be. Therefore, when the weight she places on other people's opinions is diminished, so is her performance anxiety, which will then help her let go and be herself. One of the key elements to having good sex is to be relaxed and let go of inhibitions, so when the woman is not restricting herself due to fear of judgment or failure, she can enjoy it more fully.

Letting go also means expressing herself freely, and that could look like being comfortable dancing or singing in front of people, even if she does not consider herself to be a good dancer or singer. It could also look like allowing herself to laugh out loud or even cry in public or with others around. Letting herself go means immersing herself in what she is doing and enjoying it fully, without worrying about what could go wrong or what might happen. Many of these women have trouble doing some or all of these, and so in order for them to create that internal shift, they need to start breaking down some of those inhibitions in different areas in their lives, not just during sex.

One of the ways I explore this with my clients is I ask them to think of situations in life or previous moments in which they felt they were truly immersed in what they were doing and were deeply engaged, to the extent that their self-evaluation or the evaluation of others was not of a concern to them in those moments. Activities like creative arts, music, dancing, or even being in nature hiking, or being with their pet or specific people, might give us some insight into what types of experiences help them let go. That way we can also discuss what was different about them and how they changed their mindset or behaviors in a way that allowed them to be present and just experience what IS rather than what SHOULD be happening.

Control and letting go are two opposing forces. While we try to control our emotions, behaviors, and thoughts, we only have so much control over those of others and the external world. This brings me to another trait that I find to be frequently challenging for women with vaginismus: patience. And that means not only having patience with others, but also with themselves. This relates to the previous point around placing high or unrealistic expectations onto themselves. I noticed that many of my clients felt frustrated easily when things were not happening as quickly as they wanted them to, and that applied even to some of the exercises they were working on in treatment. However, by trying to force or speed things up, they would often end up experiencing more challenges or difficulties along the way. This is why I believe it is extremely important for us clinicians to be aware of this and not collude with the client and "rush the process" either. Therapy is a great opportunity for them to learn to develop more patience, for as we know, therapy is a process that requires time, dedication, and trust. Learning to "trust the process" in this case is not only a cliché statement about therapy, but also a true growth opportunity that is very much relevant to the client's life.

Case Example

> Khuloud is a 24 year-old woman from the UAE who has been married to a distant cousin for a few months, and like many couples in her culture, they did not have any physical or sexual contact prior to the marriage. She was making great progress with her solo genital exposure progressions (explained in Chapter 5). After only a few sessions together she overcame some of her fears of inserting her finger and felt relieved and excited about her achievement. One week during our session, she expressed her frustration with not being able to progress further and insert two fingers. I asked her several questions around what she tried, how she tried it, what she did to relax her body, and how she dealt with the "stuckness," and I noticed that she was attempting to do too many things at the same time. She had already accomplished inserting a finger two weeks ago, and within the same week, she tried inserting two fingers, and three fingers, even when she was not able to fully insert two fingers yet. As soon as she made any slight progress, she would immediately attempt to go further within the same practice session, only to find herself tired, frustrated, and even sore the next day. I became concerned that her body was going to continue to associate any activity around her genitals with frustration or negative experiences, and so I firmly encouraged her to slow down. My recommendation was for her to end the practice session wherever she made small progress, and to repeat the same experience once or twice again in the next few days before continuing to push further. She just needed a reminder to be patient with herself and celebrate the small victories, even if that meant that her treatment might take slightly longer. Learning to do that with the exercises is also a metaphor for reinforcing having more patience in other areas in life.

Additionally, letting go means allowing herself to be vulnerable. It is common for such women to find it difficult to open up to people, even their partners, and share things that make them feel weak, helpless, or exposed to potentially getting hurt. As scary as it may feel, opening up to one's partner is a powerful process in learning to let go and connect deeply. This ties into the metaphors of sex and vaginismus explored earlier and how the fear of being judged, abandoned, or consumed may be at the root of the issue, and how differentiating oneself from others and setting healthy boundaries can allow for more authentic and meaningful connections. In order for the client to do that, she must firstly have a strong sense of self, and secondly, trust her partner, of course, and feel safe that he will not hurt or judge her. As a result, it is crucial for some of our work to incorporate the partner, or to at least address ways to build more trust and safety in the relationship, which will be discussed in Chapter 4.

4 Relational Factors

As discussed so far, individual factors contribute to the development of GPPPD, in addition to the types of sexual messages and education the woman assimilates and integrates throughout her life. Though vaginismus is often viewed as a sexual dysfunction that is experienced by the woman and thus treated accordingly, what I have seen is that some of the relationship dynamics and factors also play an impactful role. Therefore, my approach in working with GPPPD (and most sexual difficulties) usually incorporates gaining a deeper understanding into how the partner's behaviors, responses, and views around sex and relationships may be contributing to, maintaining, or exacerbating the issue. I tend to view sexual difficulties relationally, and find that doing so not only positively influences the treatment process, but also helps the woman feel less blamed or inadequate when they both understand how the relational factors play into their issue as opposed to viewing it purely as a personal problem or failure.

As we are establishing throughout this book, feeling safe (psychologically and physically) is fundamental for a woman to overcome her fears and be able to finally enjoy an intimate sexual relationship with her partner. A huge part of feeling safe, in order to be able to let go of inhibitions, is the ability to trust her partner and their relationship. Trust comes in many forms, such as trusting that they are loyal and faithful, trusting their judgments and decisions, trusting that they are able to handle difficult situations together, and trusting that they will be emotionally available and present for them (among other things). With all of that in mind, I believe it is very important for the woman's partner to collaborate with her in this process so that they can create the safety and connection they both need and want.

I think it is important to acknowledge that though many of us in the field support and encourage sex to be "safe," the assumption that it can be completely safe may be unfounded as it is not always a black or white concept. One cannot necessarily diminish this factor to simply being measured as either "safe" or "unsafe," but rather it is a continuum, like many other concepts in life, that is multifaceted and complex. The other point here is that the context and requirements to feeling "safe" in sex can vary from one culture to another and between individuals, and so there may not be one formula to create the safety needed for everyone. Sex might always have some element of "risk" as it can be a vulnerable experience, and it is partly the "risks" that we take that make or keep sex exciting. Having said that, I believe that the level of risk should be a healthy one. Therefore, rather than striving for what we think is completely "safe" for everyone, it may be more helpful to work toward creating the environment that for each particular client is "safe enough." For women with penetration disorders, there may always be some degree of anxiety or fear with sex, but the aim is to work toward that level being healthy that she feels she is able to get through or overcome.

Though this book is not about couples therapy per se, I have described some of the main themes I work with when treating vaginismus or working with couples in general that can help build a stronger foundation of trust and connection in the relationship. I believe that the relational work is even more important to incorporate when dealing with couples who are in an arranged marriage or who did not have sufficient opportunities prior to the marriage to be emotionally intimate. There is no particular order for the suggestions below as I often integrate some or all of them during my sessions depending on the flow and the needs of that particular client or couple. As always, I encourage the clinician to incorporate any or all of the concepts discussed here based on his/her knowledge and intuition and the specific needs of each client.

The Effect on and Role of the Partner

Penetration difficulties do not only impact the client herself; they also have an effect on the partner and could potentially put a strain on the relationship. One can understand that the partners may feel inadequate, helpless, and frustrated as well. They may also be confused at first about what is happening and why they are unable to consummate their marriage, and potentially question and blame themselves. Keep in mind that the partners themselves are often sexually inexperienced with other women prior to the marriage, especially in arranged marriages or traditional cultures, and so they may not be familiar with sexual difficulties. They may also feel conflicted regarding how best to approach sex and how they can help their partner feel less afraid, while at the same time managing their desire to have sex with their spouse. They may attempt different types of touch or sexual behaviors only to be turned down, thus potentially contributing to their lack of sexual confidence and to feeling more rejected. The emotional impact the partner experiences could contribute to how the couple deals with their difficulties, how often they attempt vaginal penetrative sex, and of course, how they relate to one another outside of the bedroom.

In addition to paying attention to how the partner may be emotionally affected, I believe it is important to assess the partner's sexual history and function, as it is not unusual for the partner to experience sexual difficulties as well. I have noticed that, often in my work, the partners of my primary clients tend to be "convenient" in that they also (knowingly or unknowingly) suffer from either sexual dysfunction or shame or anxiety around sex. What happens in the particular situation of vaginismus then is that, since the partners may also have some anxiety around sex, that enables them to not be pushy about it and instead be quite sympathetic toward the vaginismic woman. For the vaginismic woman, it is convenient to have a partner that is avoidant of sex as well. At the same time, the fears or difficulties that the vaginismic woman suffers from are convenient for the vaginismic partner who also suffers from sexual dysfunction or anxiety, as the avoidance of sex "protects" him from having to confront his own fears of failure or sexual problems. One study showed that the partners of the vaginismic women had little or no sexual experience prior to the current relationship, the majority of them had never had penetrative sex, were not provided with any sex education in the families of origin, and were raised in a culture where sex was considered taboo. In addition, erectile dysfunction was found to be a common sexual difficulty that the partner experienced, and may have shown signs of avoidance of sex prior to the marriage (Klein et al., 2015). Therefore, gathering a detailed history of the partner's sexual experience, views, and feelings would be significant and extremely beneficial in order to address the avoidance of sex in both partners and to support the man in building more confidence sexually as well.

Though only a small percentage of my clients' partners suffered from their own sexual dysfunctions (erectile dysfunction and premature ejaculation being the most common ones), I think it is still crucial for the partner's emotional and sexual wellbeing to be taken into account and addressed appropriately. If the partner also suffers from a sexual dysfunction, then the therapy needs to incorporate strategies for the male client to resolve his performance anxiety and overcome his difficulties. Not being able to achieve or maintain an erection sufficient for penetration could make vaginal intercourse even more challenging and therefore exacerbate the issue. If the partner suffers from performance anxiety, that could be contributing to the lack of confidence the couple is feeling during sexual activities, which may not help the woman feel safer and more relaxed. At times it may be more effective and appropriate for the partner to address his sexual dysfunction with a different practitioner (sex therapist, urologist, or sexual medicine doctor, depending on the situation). However, I believe it is useful for the woman to be involved in his treatment as well, if the clinician deems it more appropriate for the partner to work with a different practitioner. The Sensate Focus program described later in this book is an approach I often incorporate while working with men with sexual difficulties, and so that may be one of the ways I would work toward addressing both partners' sexual dysfunctions at the same time. The therapist should be the judge of how to work with both sexual difficulties.

Interestingly, one study has shown that partners of women with dyspareunia reported more negative reactions to the woman's pain than partners of women with lifelong vaginismus, who tended to show more concerned and caring behaviors. At the same time, women with dyspareunia showed more task-persistence behavior, meaning that they would persist with vaginal intercourse despite it being painful, while women with vaginismus showed more fear-avoidance behaviors, meaning they would avoid sex due to the fear of pain. Women with dyspareunia also showed fewer pleasure motives and more "duty" motives for sex, which may be why they would continue to engage in sex even when it is painful. Women with vaginismus engaged in less contact with the penis such as giving oral sex compared to controls most likely as a way to reduce the chance that physical contact might lead to vaginal penetrative sex (Brauer et al., 2014).

What also tends to happen with women who suffer from vulvodynia (vulvar pain) is that the partners with more solicitous responses (i.e., who show more sympathy, attention, and support) perpetuate this avoidance cycle by stopping sexual activity because of the pain. Partners with negative responses such as criticism or hostility also reinforce this cycle. It has been shown, however, that partners with facilitative responses – meaning who are encouraging to the woman's efforts at adapting and coping with the pain – may help in decreasing the pain (Rosen et al., 2012; McNicoll et al., 2016). Results of McNicoll et al. (2016) also suggest that women with pain tend to communicate more openly about their sexual preferences and needs during sex (in other words, are more sexually assertive) when they perceive their partner as being facilitative (i.e., demonstrating more coping behaviors and affection during sexual activity).

Given the importance I have ascribed throughout this book to a woman learning to be more assertive in the relationship in order for her to feel more empowered and relaxed, it would be very useful to work on the interpersonal factors to help the partner learn to adopt more adaptive and affectionate responses, as opposed to simply avoiding sex out of sympathy. That way he can provide her with the encouraging environment she needs to feel more comfortable asserting herself. Relating this to my observations of my clients, the majority of the partners of my clients who were suffering from vaginismus or penetration phobia tended to show more compassion and concern, without pressuring the woman to "go through with it," meaning more solicitous responses. My clients generally confirmed that by describing their partners to be understanding, patient, and sympathetic toward them regarding their fears or sexual difficulties. While this is helpful in that it does not push the woman to suffer and endure a painful or traumatic experience, it also serves as a maintaining factor as the avoidance cycle of sex continues. In addition, the woman avoiding other forms of sexual contact can negatively impact the relationship as a whole as it diminishes opportunities for them to create and develop sexual intimacy. With these points in mind, I believe it is important to create a safe, trusting, and cooperative relationship where the couple learns to adapt to the fears and progressively overcome them together rather than to react negatively to them or avoid them altogether.

58   Relational Factors

Case Example

Ayesha is 23 years old, from Sudan, and has been married to her husband for two months. Their marriage was a love marriage, and they were not sexually active before marriage. From the early days of their relationship, they experienced some conflict as they disagreed on some values. They immediately encountered difficulties when attempting to consummate their marriage. Though the majority of my clients' husbands were understanding and patient, Ayesha's husband unfortunately did not deal with their sexual struggles well and would get very angry with each unsuccessful attempt. She expressed feeling very judged, criticized, and pressured by him about sex. It was evident that this was a case of emotional and verbal abuse as she felt emotionally intimidated. She sometimes felt the abuse was justified because she believed it was "her fault" that they could not have sex. As a therapist, I did not feel it would be ethical for me to suggest that she continues to progress with the exercises and partner exercises while she does not feel emotionally safe in the relationship. The focus of our sessions thus shifted for a while to address her relationship concerns and work through her options regarding how to deal with the abuse. Learning to set boundaries when it was safe to do so and empowering her internally so that she feels she does not deserve to be treated that way were some of the main themes we were working on at that stage.

Another way the partner may be unintentionally reinforcing or maintaining the woman's lack of assertiveness or confidence in the relationship is by lacking assertiveness and authenticity himself. Clearly, being aggressive/hostile as in the previous case example is not the answer, nor is being avoidant. I think that her partner learning to be more assertive, on the other hand, can not only help him feel more confident, but also help her view him as a more confident and secure partner. One of the key points I keep coming back to is the importance of the client trusting in her partner. Trust partly means knowing that he cares for her, respects her boundaries, and will be there for her emotionally. Trust also comes from knowing that he is reliable, responsible, and assertive. For example, if the client's partner is someone who tends to be more passive and does not stand up for himself, she might not trust that he is able to take care of things when she needs him to. In order for her to let go of some control, it helps for her to feel safe in his ability to take charge.

As mentioned previously, it was quite common that women who have sought therapy with me for vaginismus were married to men who were very understanding and patient. Though having a compassionate and supportive partner is extremely beneficial in the process of her overcoming her difficulties, I do not believe it is helpful for her to be with someone who allows anything and everything and does not set boundaries or speak up. I think this can create some anxiety around being "intruded upon," which is a factor we have established is often involved in women with vaginismus. If a woman has difficulty with letting people in because she has experienced people in her life as intrusive, controlling, or overbearing, it will be more difficult to feel safe and relaxed if her partner is not able to set boundaries and protect the relationship from that.

Just as it is important for her partner to learn to assert himself, it is equally important for her to let go of some control to allow him to do that. As we explore this topic in sessions, I would discuss how she can learn to allow him to take initiative in more decisions and plans so that she can learn to see him as an authentic individual, and as a reliable and trustworthy partner. By giving him the space to share his needs and requests and set his boundaries, he can build his own confidence and assertiveness and be a model for her to do that as well. Of course, I am not suggesting that it becomes an unbalanced relationship where he is in total control, but what I am suggesting is for them to learn to differentiate from one another, and to be authentic and assertive individuals, in order for them to trust in themselves and each other. When she can see her partner as a solid and authentic individual, she will feel more secure in letting go with him.

Connecting this concept with previous themes around the woman being an authentic and assertive individual, the relationship I encourage couples to work toward looks like two differentiated individuals who stand on their own solid feet and are connected at the same time. We must be careful that being assertive does not look like making decisions for the other person or treating the other person like an inferior. It is about empowering both partners to hold on to their own selves and be connected at the same time. One of the books I highly recommend that explores the concept of differentiation, authenticity, intimacy, and connection, is *Passionate Marriage*, by David Schnarch. Meaningful connection is not a constant experience, it happens in moments; couples ebb and flow between separateness and connection. As Gibran Khalil Gibran said, "Let there be spaces in your togetherness."

Case Example

> *Fatima and Adnan, who were of Pakistani origin and living in the UAE, have been together many years and love each other. They have been married for four years and were still unable to consummate their marriage. There had been many contributing and precipitating factors, in addition to some sexual trauma and difficulties that Adnan had experienced, so it was quite multilayered. However, one thing I noticed during our couple's sessions was that Fatima seemed to rely quite a bit on Adnan to make decisions – she would often ask him for advice and have difficulty making up her own mind. This put him in a parental role where she would come to him for advice and he would guide her, which of course came from a good place, but ultimately disempowered her in the relationship and made her quite dependent on him. I suggested that he change the way he responds to her advice-seeking behaviors and work on allowing her to make up her own mind. This could look like him offering more questions rather than solutions or simply mirroring back to her what she said. That way she could think through the options and solutions herself while she is in dialogue with him instead of depending on him to provide the answers. This is one of the ways she can start*

differentiating herself from him and create a healthier dynamic that involves two adults. They worked on it, and this helped them be less codependent, grow, and see each other more as adults.

The Relationship Foundation

In the early stages of therapy with couples, I usually have discussions around their relationship values, goals, and visions. This helps them gain deeper awareness into themselves and each other, and create opportunities to connect and grow. I like having these conversations early on in the couple's therapy process because I feel it opens up deeper discussions about their needs, wants, and fears in a safe and non-confrontational way. By mediating these types of dialogue, I provide them with an opportunity to firstly get to know each other on a deeper level and create connection, and secondly, practice having meaningful or potentially difficult conversations together.

One of the things I do is to guide them through a progressive muscular relaxation practice in the session, followed by a visualization practice. In this exercise, I ask them to fast-forward into the future and imagine the ideal relationship they want to achieve after they have finished the therapy, and to pay attention to what organically comes up for them in terms of visuals, settings, and feelings. As they continue to hold that vision in mind, I ask them to focus on what it is about themselves that is different in that image. The point here is that I am beginning to help them create those mental pathways and possibilities to the relationship that they want, and to encourage each partner to look inwards and take some responsibility for what they can change in order to achieve the relationship they want, as opposed to just focusing on the problem and what the partner has to do differently. I believe this visualization is inspired by Imago therapy, which is one of my favorite approaches to incorporate when working with couples. After this exercise, we discuss in the session what they each saw, what it means to them, and how they each feel about their partner's vision. Just as athletes use visualization to strengthen the neural pathways in their brain and improve their performance, so clients can use visualization to train their minds to create more behaviors that will improve their relationship and help them be more intentional.

Case Example

In one of my early sessions with Dalia and Ali (a couple originally from Saudi Arabia living in the UAE), Dalia shared that during the visualization exercise she envisioned them walking together on a beach, all dressed in white. As I explored further, it was revealed that the meaning behind that vision for her revolved around being relaxed, playful, and connected. When she was asked to focus on herself in that image, she said she realized that in order for them to achieve that, she needs to work on reducing her anxiety and being more present. I have found many times that both partners share similar desires even if their vision might look a little different. For example, Ali here did not see them on a beach, but instead they were at home together. However, the meaning behind his vision was similar in that he also wanted more connection and peace at home, and what he needed to change was for him to be more affectionate and expressive.

Along the same lines, I would explore in sessions what their main relationship values are by asking them to list, in order of importance, what is most important to each of them in a marriage or long-term relationship. I usually go through this verbally with clients in the session, and it gives us an opportunity to notice how similar their values are, and how they feel about each other's values and needs. I, of course, go into more depth as I would ask them to elaborate on what each value means to them, why it is important, how much they believe their actions are aligned with it, and how they would feel if that value was not honored in the relationship. For example, for one partner, fun might be an important value in a marriage, and for the other partner not so much. In situations like this I think it would be helpful to get a better understanding of what counts as "fun" for that partner, why fun is important, and what they are afraid would happen if the marriage was not as fun as they would like it to be.

We might be able to find some commonalities between the two where they share the same meaning of fun and are both interested in experiencing together. If not, then we might be able to negotiate other ways to incorporate fun into the partner's life even if that does not directly involve the partner. I do not believe there is one right way to resolve these types of disagreements — it is very common for any two individuals to disagree on things that may never be fully resolved. I do believe, however, that it is important to negotiate alternative solutions, and if none are to be found, to then work on whether or not that disagreement is something the partner or couple can live with or change their perspective on. In the case of "fun," for example, maybe the fear is that the partner will get bored and leave them, and so it may be helpful to address the core issue here, reframe "fun" and "boredom," and learn about different ways to keep things exciting in a relationship.

Another main exploration I go through with the majority of the couples I work with is discussing the traits and behaviors they like about each other, the behaviors they do not like about each other, and what they would like to change or improve. Credit needs to be given to my supervisor Jean Miller for developing this exercise and to Judi Keshet-Orr and my Psychosexual Diploma training for providing me with it. I find this helpful to address any relationship frustrations or areas of conflict that the couple may be struggling with and unable to resolve. Additionally, having these dialogues in sessions helps build the skills and confidence around discussing difficult topics together. Being able to confront difficult subjects and negotiate agreements together is like a muscle that requires training and strengthening. Lastly, this exercise provides the clients with the opportunity to really think about the qualities they appreciate about each other, to help them see the good, and to verbalize that to one another. They are asked to answer these questions separately at home and to bring their answers to the sessions so that we can constructively discuss them.

I ask them to list:

- The four things they were attracted to in the beginning of their relationship, whether it was physical or personality traits.
- The four things they were unsure of or hesitant about in the beginning of their relationship.
- The four to six things they really like about their partner in the present relationship.
- The four to six things they do not like about their partner.
- The four to six requests for change.

Using some of the communication guidelines discussed next, we explore these points over a few sessions, and I would moderate a dialogue between them as they express to each other what they wrote. I would help them continue to reinforce active listening skills and to positively frame their complaints. For example, I would emphasize that they avoid judging personality traits when it comes to the complaints and to instead describe specific behaviors that they do not like. Also, I support them in making clear, measurable, and positive requests for change.

At first glance this exercise seems pretty straightforward and specific, and it can absolutely be done in that way and address the points laid out. However, what I love about this exercise and the way I usually go about it is to use the questions and themes that come up as a gateway to unraveling more profound conversations and additional layers to the couple's needs and wounds. For example, one of my clients shared that one of the things she loves the most about her husband is that he is grounded. As we explored further what that meant to her, and how he perceived that quality in himself, we revealed that he finds dealing with and expressing vulnerability difficult, and that he always needed to keep things under control growing up. That led to us exploring how showing vulnerability could help them connect on a deeper level and me facilitating some moments in sessions where they were able to make that kind of emotional contact with each other.

Case Example

In one of our sessions, Zena expressed that she feels frustrated that her husband, Ramy, does not accommodate his plans for her or others. If we take this point at face value, we can work on helping Ramy acknowledge her feelings and needs and negotiate when and how they can adjust their behaviors to resolve this. Sometimes that is all that is needed to address the issue. However, when I dug a little deeper into it and asked Zena to elaborate on what Ramy's lack of flexibility meant to her, Ramy described an example that shed some light on the situation. That helped her realize that when he chooses his own comfort over other people's desires, it leads to them spending less time together, and that what Zena really wants is to spend more time with him. This revealed that what is underneath her frustration around his "selfishness" lies her need and desire for connection with him. That was a revelation for him, and once he understood that, he realized that it is not such a trivial matter after all, and expressed that he was also interested in spending more time together.

One other main pillar for a healthy and happy relationship is feeling loved and appreciated. As we are building or solidifying the foundation of the clients' relationship, I like to explore how they each feel loved and valued, and how much they express affection and appreciation to each other. After being together for a long time, it is not uncommon for couples to show less appreciation and focus more on the complaints, thus potentially affecting the emotional connection and romance in the relationship. The book *The Five Love Languages* by Gary Chapman is a popular one that thoroughly explains the five different ways through which people express and feel love. I would encourage clients to read this book to get a better sense of what they each need to feel loved and appreciated. The book describes that similarly to speaking different languages, people show love and need love in different ways. Often, two people in a relationship have different love languages, which may result in one or both of them not feeling loved enough, when in reality, all that is happening is that they are speaking different languages and not getting through to each other.

Here is a brief description of what the five love languages are with examples based on an internet meme I once saw:

- Verbal Affirmations: verbally expressing love, affection, and appreciation. "The tacos you made are delicious, thank you!"
- Physical Touch: showing affection through physical contact such as hugging, kissing, touching, and sex. "I want to wrap and hold you like a taco."
- Quality Time: spending time together where you are engaged with each other, doing something fun or meaningful together. "Let's make tacos together."
- Acts of Service: doing something for your partner such as cooking, running errands, fixing things around the house, planning activities for them, etc. "I made you tacos."
- Gifts: they do not have to be expensive gifts, but simply the act of getting something for your partner counts. "I brought you tacos."

Usually, we all need and show different degrees of all of the love languages, but we tend to have one or two that are dominant. For example, though the client might enjoy quality time, the thing she needs the most that makes her feel most loved might be verbal affirmations. Her partner might share the same language, which would make things easier, but he may not. In situations where they speak different languages, I like to discuss the importance of understanding better what each partner's main emotional needs are, and to encourage them to speak them more often. For example, if her partner feels most loved when she does things for him, but acts of service is not her main language, then loving her partner means making conscious efforts to do more things for him (they could make a list of things the partner enjoys such as cooking for him, or running his errands, and set reminders to do them more often). The same applies to other love languages and the other way around of course.

Communication Skills

Healthy communication is key in a successful and happy marriage, or even, in my opinion, in any inter-personal relationship. I have had many clients say in sessions that their partner should know what they mean because they have expressed it one way or another. Heck, I am sure I have probably thought so or said so myself! The fact that we have said something does not automatically mean that our partner has understood it. Sometimes we do not even say things directly, but assume that our partners should know from our body language and indirect messages we have sent. And of course, sometimes we say things in a critical or blaming way that makes it difficult for our partner to receive it well and respond to it constructively, and so they become defensive. Learning to communicate effectively not only helps the couple resolve disagreements, express their needs and feelings more clearly, and connect more deeply, it also helps them build assertiveness, which as discussed in this chapter and in Chapter 3, is a skill that I think can tremendously help both partners build more confidence and trust.

There are a few fundamental and clear tips on how to speak and listen effectively that the majority of couples therapists would coach couples on (some of which are described below), in order to promote a deeper understanding and connection between the couple. Some of the suggestions I offer below are based on the Imago dialogue. To learn more about that or go deeper into the details of the Imago dialogue and approach, I suggest reading the works and books of Harville Hendrix, PhD, and Helen LaKelly Hunt, PhD (such as *Getting the Love You Want*, and *Keeping the Love You Find*).

<u>Active Listening Worksheet</u>

- <u>Set a time for dialogue:</u> *sometimes when we want to discuss an important subject with our partner, we spontaneously bring it up at a time that is not the most conducive to having a calm and focused conversation. Our partner may be tired, busy, not mentally available, or simply not in the mood to have a profound discussion. When we bring up a serious issue at the wrong time, we might be met with dismissive responses, defensiveness, or frustration, which can lead to conflict and be less encouraging for future conversations. As a result, one of the first things we can do to prepare for a constructive conversation is to plan it. Ask your partner when would be a good time to*

discuss something important and set aside that time together where you are both present (remove distractions such as phones, TV, etc.).
- _Practice self-soothing and grounding:_ this is especially important for the listener since they may be receiving information that might be triggering. Before your assigned time, take a few minutes to practice one of the breathing/grounding exercises in order to enter the conversation either as the speaker or listener in a calm manner.
- _Mirroring:_ as the listener, listen without interruption, set aside your opinion for the moment, and when the speaker is done, just repeat back to him/her a summary of what you understood they said, and then check if they feel understood. For example, it could sound like "I heard you say that (paraphrase what you understood) ... Did I get you?" or, "I understand that (paraphrase what you understood) ... is that right?" Though it is common for people to think about how to defend their point of view when listening, at this stage in the dialogue, it is not about defending your opinion or proving who or what is right. It is about making sure you understand what your partner is saying. If your partner feels understood, they say something like "Yes," or "You got me," and if they do not, they can reiterate and clarify the part that you missed or misunderstood. After that, you can ask, "Is there more?" to give them the opportunity to express anything that may be left.

One client once expressed a very common type of conflict that many people end up arguing about – driving! She said to her partner in the session that she feels scared when he speeds. The husband responded, as many of us would, by arguing that he does not think he speeds and that his driving is not dangerous. This exemplifies how many of us often listen with the intent to defend ourselves or prove that we are right as opposed to listening with the intent to understand. In order to help him understand her feelings better and improve their communication overall, I asked him to just listen and put his own opinions about his driving aside, and to repeat back to her what he understood. This is hard for many of us to do, but by remembering that the intention is to understand, he was able to do so. Once clients become more comfortable with mirroring, they can move on to learning how to validate each other.

- _Validation:_ validating the speaker means expressing to them that what they are feeling makes sense. Sometimes we just want to feel acknowledged, and to know that we are not crazy for feeling or thinking what we do. Once you have successfully mirrored your partner, try to put yourself in his/her shoes to see that from their perspective, what they are feeling is valid. Going back to the driving example, when the husband insisted that his driving is not dangerous, I asked him to imagine himself someone who sees his driving as fast and dangerous, and to think about whether or not it makes sense for someone in that position to feel scared, regardless of whether or not his driving actually is dangerous. When he was able to do that, he validated his wife's feelings and said that he can understand how she would feel scared in that situation. In their case, the thing that upset the wife the most about this issue was not his driving as much as it was that she felt her feelings were not taken seriously. This was probably the first time she heard him acknowledge that her feelings are valid.

One analogy I sometimes offer clients who have difficulty accepting that others may view their behavior differently than they do is comparing their conflict to going for a massage. Let us say that the person getting a massage likes soft and gentle pressure and asks the massage therapist for that. The massage therapist conducts the massage with what he/she considers soft pressure. The person getting the massage may have tender muscles and experience the massage very differently as the pressure feels quite hard and uncomfortable, and so they tell the massage therapist that the pressure is hard and ask for a more gentle approach. Who is right in this situation? How do we define soft or hard pressure? The person giving the massage thinks they are being soft, while the person receiving it is impacted very differently. To me, this is an example of how each behavior and experience is subjective, and so though the person giving/doing might have the best of intentions, their behavior can still have a very different and sometimes negative impact on others.

- *Empathy:* once you are able to expand your view and affirm the other person's perspective, you can take validation a little further and empathize with your partner. It is much easier to understand and empathize with what the other person is feeling if you share a similar experience, and it becomes more challenging when you react differently to a similar event. For example, if you have a pet that you love deeply and you know someone who just lost a pet, you can easily imagine how devastated they may be about their loss. It will not be difficult for you to say something like: "I can imagine you must be heartbroken." On the other hand, if your partner is upset about something a co-worker said and you normally tend to easily separate between work and your personal life, it may be more challenging for you to empathize with their feelings and you may be more inclined to say something like: "Don't let work get to you" or "Who cares about what they think, just let it go."

When we are able to truly empathize with someone, we take the conversation to a level beyond the information being exchanged and into a place of emotional connection. We are not only helping the speaker feel understood; we are also making them feel seen and accepted. Some people find it easier to empathize with others, and though this sounds stereotypical, women tend to value empathy more than men. Though it may not be a natural or automatic way for some of you to respond, I do believe it is a skill we can learn and build. One of the perspectives I offer to clients to help them empathize is to imagine a child feeling frustrated or upset about something that, to us adults, seems like such a trivial thing, but to that child might mean the world. This just portrays how two people can feel very differently about the same situation based on their experience and view of the world. Another approach would be to ask the person who is unable to empathize to think of a different situation in their life that made them feel the same way, and to realize that their partner is going through the same feelings just in response to a different situation. For example, if someone cannot empathize with the loss of a pet, maybe they can relate to the feeling of the loss of a family member, and that will help them understand what the other person is going through.

Often, we listen with the intent to respond or defend ourselves, which can then lead to the conflict intensifying or turning into a power struggle, thus leaving the initial subject of disagreement unresolved. I have found that many times actively listening to your partner and empathizing with them is all they need to overcome what they are feeling, and sometimes the actual subject of the conversation does not matter as much as the ability to have a supportive and validating experience and an emotional connection. Other times, however, the subject needs a resolution, or at the very least, an exchange of thoughts and emotions around it. And so, though it may be natural to think of your defense or response when listening to someone, holding back from immediately replying with an argument is extremely helpful.

This does not mean that you are never allowed to share your opinion or explain the situation from your perspective, it just means that you should choose better timing. Work on reflecting back what you understood from your partner to make them feel heard first, and then once they feel validated, you may then go on to explain your point of view and express your concerns or feelings around the subject. Remember that most of the time there are no facts, but simply different perspectives and experiences. So while you may experience a certain situation in one way (for example, leaving dirty clothes lying around is frustrating to you, but not to him), your partner may view it in a completely different way that may have more or less of an emotional impact on him, depending on his history and personality.

In order to make it easier on the listener to empathize and listen without getting defensive, the speaker must relay the message in a calm and clear way without blaming. The Assertiveness Training Worksheet in Chapter 3 provides some guidelines that are useful for healthy communication – here are some reminders and suggestions for the speaker:

<u>Healthy Communication Worksheet</u>

- <u>Start sentences with "I" rather than "You"</u>: this way you are explaining how you see the situation and feel about it instead of accusing the person of wrongdoing or judging them.
- <u>Be specific</u>: focus on the specific behavior that you do not like as opposed to judging a general quality or trait in the person negatively. Clearly explain how that behavior made you feel and what it meant to you.
- <u>Make a request for change</u>: it would help the listener tremendously if you can enlighten them on what you would prefer instead so that they know what they can do differently next time.

> For example, instead of saying "You're so lazy," say something along the lines of "When you leave your clothes lying around it really frustrates me because it makes me think that my presence does not matter to you. I would really prefer it if you would please pick them up and put them in the dirty laundry basket in future."
>
> Similarly to the previous suggestions on mirroring, the listener will then paraphrase back what they heard to check if they understood: "So I heard you say that you feel frustrated when I leave dirty clothes lying around, and you would like me to place them in the laundry basket instead. Did I get you?" This is where you will respond with "Yes, thank you for listening." And if your partner is not willing or able to fulfill your request, they can suggest another solution that would help resolve your frustration.

Following these general and common guidelines can help couples speak with and listen to each other in a more focused, clear, and structured way so that they create a safe container to be vulnerable with each other. Maintaining eye contact and holding hands while they are having a meaningful or difficult conversation can also help to keep the warmth and connection, thus making it more difficult to get angry at each other. I usually encourage couples to dedicate time each week where they are present and relaxed to "check in" with each other and share appreciations, desires and hopes, and requests for change. I find that it is especially important in our busy modern world to commit to regular "check ins" with each other to nurture the relationship, otherwise time can easily get away and couples can end up spending weeks or months without having focused and meaningful conversations.

5 Mastering Her Body

While we are working on modifying some of the common negative and unhelpful sexual beliefs and misconceptions associated with sexual anxiety and shame, and creating a healthy balance of differentiation and trust and connection in the relationship, one of the most important parts of therapy is to support the client through getting to know her body. Some of the main goals behind practicing these exercises are to enable her to feel more comfortable with her sexuality and genitals through self-exploration, and then for her to overcome her fear of penetration by safely and gradually getting exposed to different types of vaginal penetration. Self-exploration also helps in adopting a more positive body image as many women tend to have a negative view of their bodies, which contributes to feelings of discomfort in sexual activities. For example, it was found that people with more negative evaluations of their appearance reported more self-conscious appearance concerns during sexual activity, and women reported higher levels than men of self-conscious focus on their bodies and desires to conceal certain parts of their bodies during sexual activities (La Rocque & Cioe, 2011). That study also found that men and women who reported a more negative body image are more likely to avoid sexual activity than those with a more positive body image. Usually, I start the client on the physical exercises soon after we begin therapy, and so often what happens is that she practices the exercises at home, alongside us working through some of the unhealthy sexual beliefs and relational dynamics in sessions. The exercises tend to bring up many of the emotional, relational, and psychological concepts we will be exploring anyway, and so I find that it is useful for her to be behaviorally and experientially working through the topics we are processing in sessions.

Pelvic Floor Strengthening

One of the ways for the client to learn to be more connected to her vaginal muscles and to strengthen them is to train them through Kegel exercises. Dr. Arnold Kegel developed some exercises in 1952 for women who were suffering from urinary incontinence and similar problems. It was found that the pelvic floor muscles in these women were weak and not functioning properly, and that exercising them not only eliminated their

DOI: 10.4324/9781003129172-5

medical problems, but also increased their potential for genital sensation and orgasm (Heiman & LoPiccolo, 1988, p. 51). The reason I think it is helpful for women with vaginismus to practice Kegel exercises is so that they can learn to control their pelvic muscles and consequently intentionally relax them when they are getting tense during sexual activities. Kegel exercises can be done anywhere, anytime, and I strongly recommend that they practice them during the genital exposure progressions discussed later. Though pelvic floor specialists tend to advise against actually practicing this while urinating, the simplest way I explain this exercise to clients is for them to imagine themselves urinating and then wanting to stop the flow. In that situation, they would contract their vaginal and pelvic muscles to stop the flow. Then, imagine wanting to let go and continue urinating, they will then relax their pelvic muscles in order to release. They should feel their vaginal area tightening up and relaxing when they practice this.

Kegel Exercise Guideline

Practice contracting your pelvic muscles for a few seconds and then relaxing them for a few seconds, over a few minutes every day. This can be done anytime, while standing, sitting, or lying down (a word of caution here as it is not recommended to do Kegels while on the toilet). Practice different rhythms, such as contracting and holding them for three to five seconds followed by three to five seconds of relaxation. Contract the muscles while inhaling, as if you are pulling your pelvic muscles upward as you take the breath in. This may be a little more challenging as you may tend to contract your stomach as well. With practice you will learn to separate between the pelvic muscles and stomach muscles and keep your stomach relaxed while contracting your vaginal muscles. At other times, alternate, and contract and relax your muscles quickly like a fast pulse while breathing regularly. Practice these exercises for a few minutes each day. At first, they may require some concentration, but they will become easier to practice with time that they can be done while driving, watching TV, or doing routine things. Remember to focus on what you are feeling in your genital area without any expectation of a specific sensation. Learning to tune into and gaining awareness around your genitals is part of what will help you feel more in control of your body and its responses.

(Based partly on Heiman & LoPiccolo, 1988, p. 53)

Though Kegels are exercises I do encourage my clients to practice, I would not say they are a main part of my treatment plan, and are certainly not sufficient on their own for the majority of my clients. I mostly find them to be valuable for clients with GPPPD to help them gain better control over their pelvic muscles and learn to relax their vaginal muscles during the gradual exposure exercises described later to make inserting her fingers or any object or penis easier. Strengthening the pelvic muscles can also help women be able to have orgasms and experience more intense orgasms.

For more information about Kegel exercises I would refer to a pelvic floor specialist (one expert I follow on Instagram for example is Kim Vopni: @vaginacoach who often shares tips and guidelines for Kegel exercises).

Mindfulness, Relaxation, and Grounding

Learning to manage stress and anxiety is a very useful skill in life in general, and when it comes to sexual difficulties. Mindfulness, for example, helps us reduce anxiety as we learn to focus on the present and not the past or future, and helps to enjoy the things we do more intensely. During sex, it helps us learn to be more present in the moment rather than consumed in our negative or anxious thoughts, thus making the experience more pleasurable. One of the killers of good sex is being distracted by irrelevant or negative thoughts, and so learning to be more relaxed, present, and more sensual helps to enjoy the sensations and strengthen the connection with your partner. I often recommend that my clients incorporate mindfulness and stress-management practices regularly, if they do not already do so. There are great videos on YouTube and even great Apps such as Headspace, Calm, and Insight Timer that guide the listener through meditations and mindfulness practices. Described below are various mindfulness, relaxation, breathing, and grounding practices that can help the client learn to reduce anxiety and relax.

Mindfulness in Daily Life

Do this often in various daily activities, such as when you are in the shower, having a meal, or spending time in nature. When you are in the shower, bring your attention to each of your senses, one at a time, and spend some time taking it all in. For example, listen to the sound of the water more closely, feel the sensations of the water on your skin, pay attention to the temperature of the water, look at the water and your body in detail, take in the smells of the soaps and steam. Feel some water in your mouth, the temperature, taste, texture.

When you are having a meal, instead of eating it quickly as we mostly do these days, take your time to look at it first, observing the different colors, shapes, and textures. Smell the dish and try to distinguish between the different scents. Touch it if you are up for it and feel the temperature and texture on your fingers. Pay attention to what you hear around you, can you identify certain sounds? Lastly, take your first bite and chew very slowly, taking in all the flavors, and paying attention to the texture and temperature, and of course savoring every bit of it as it melts in your mouth. The goal is to experience every sensory stimulus more intensely and attentively.

When you are walking outdoors, or sitting on the beach, practice a similar concept where you pay attention to the sounds around you, the smells, the breeze, the sun

> on your skin, touch surfaces around you, and take it in. I am fairly certain that
> you will enjoy all these experiences so much more when you immerse yourself
> into them more fully.

Becoming more mindful and focused on their sensations will help the clients with the next steps of the treatment as they learn to be more in touch with their body and attuned to what it needs.

Other practices I strongly encourage clients (and people in general) to implement in order to be more mindful and relaxed in life are relaxation and grounding exercises. These exercises are relevant to penetration difficulties in that they teach the client to relax and feel more centered, both mentally and physically, which could also help her enjoy the experience better. Before even getting to attempt penetrative sex, practicing relaxation exercises is helpful in her process of getting through the progressive exposure exercises described later. I usually guide the clients through some of the relaxation or breathing exercises during some sessions, and encourage them to practice one of them before they attempt any of the exercises and on a regular basis, in order to strengthen their ability to achieve a relaxed state.

Progressive Muscular Relaxation Exercise

> *Let's begin by finding a comfortable position, seated or lying down, and gently closing your eyes. Bring your attention to your breath, slowing it down, and focusing on taking long deep breaths in, and just letting the air naturally flow out. If you get distracted by irrelevant or negative thoughts, just acknowledge them, and gently bring your attention back to your breath. Every time you inhale, you are taking in more positive energy and peaceful sensations, and every time you exhale just release all the tension and negative energy. Practice taking a few long deep breaths in while imagining that your belly is a balloon, and when you inhale you are inflating that balloon as much as possible, and then just releasing your breath letting the air flow out of the balloon. Next time you inhale I'd like you to hold your breath in for as long as you can, and then let it go. Do that twice more, and each time try to hold your breath in a little longer than the last time. Notice how much more relaxed your body already feels and let yourself just sink into the chair (or ground).*

> *While keeping your eyes closed and continuing to breathe deeply, I'd like you to slowly scan your body from head to toe for any tightness or tension in your muscles. Let's begin with your head and forehead, notice any tightness there, and either mentally or physically relax it by contracting your muscles and letting them go. Move on to your eyes, then cheeks and jaw. Relax your face. Next, relax your neck and your shoulders. Relax your arms all the way down to your hands and fingers. Remember that, if mentally relaxing them is difficult, you can physically contract your muscles and then relax them if that feels better. Keep breathing deeply. Relax your chest and your upper back, and then your belly and lower back. Relax your hips, your pelvic muscles, and your glutes. Relax your thighs,*

your calves, and your legs all the way down to your ankles and toes. Your body and mind are completely relaxed. Continue to breathe for a few breaths and when you are ready, you can softly start rolling your head from side to side, or moving your fingers and toes, or stretching your body to gradually bring yourself back to the room and the present moment. When you are ready you may open your eyes.

Box Breathing Exercise

Box breathing is a simple practice that helps you focus on breathing in order to down-regulate and be present. Take a long deep breath in for four seconds, then hold it in for four seconds, then exhale for four seconds, and then hold it in for four seconds. Repeat this loop as needed until you feel relaxed and calm, or for at least four times. You can also go for seven seconds instead of four seconds in each stage. This rhythm forms the shape of a box (illustrated in Figure 5.1), hence the name.

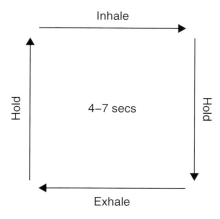

Figure 5.1 Box breathing.

Five, Four, Three, Two, One

The concept behind this one is for you to really pay attention to your sensations, one sense at a time, in order to feel more grounded. Close your eyes for most of it, preferably, and practice this one while outdoors if possible. Start with looking for five things you SEE in your environment (eyes open for this part obviously). It is important to take some time to pay attention to the objects you are noticing. Next, close your eyes, and focus on four things you HEAR. After that, move on to identifying and paying attention to three things you FEEL (touching different things in your environment). Next, focus on two things you SMELL. This might be a little more difficult to do, but it can simply be the smell of your own perfume, your shampoo in your hair, the grass, and anything else you can pick up on in your environment. Lastly, try to identify one thing you TASTE, even if it is the taste of the coffee you had this morning in your mouth, or the taste of the last thing you ate, unless there is an item you can actually safely taste in your environment at that moment. For each sense, take your time, and try to look for stimuli that are less obvious as well, such as looking for objects that are further away in addition to things that are close to you, and listening to sounds that are more challenging to hear.

Self-Sensate

When I work with women experiencing difficulties with sex, very often I would focus on her individual work first, in order for her to develop a more relaxed and positive relationship with her body and sexuality. The exercises I suggest for her to practice individually are referred to as "Self-Sensate" exercises or a "Self-Sensate program." Therefore, for the remainder of the book I may be referring to the solo or individual exercises the client practices with her body as "Self-Sensate exercises." Once she has overcome her main personal obstacles with sex and feels more empowered and connected with her body and sexuality, I then start introducing the couples exercises (in Chapter 6). The body image and body exploration exercises of the Self-Sensate exercises described below were inspired by one of the books I highly recommend to women (with some modifications and additions): *Becoming Orgasmic* by Julia R. Heiman and Joseph LoPiccolo (1988). These exercises follow a progressive sequence where the client gradually and safely gets to know her body through sight and touch.

The Self-Sensate and couples sensate exercises generally follow a concept similar to the treatment of phobias called progressive desensitization or gradual exposure therapy. Progressive desensitization is a behavioral therapy that aims to remove or reduce the fear associated with a stimulus by replacing it with a relaxed state or response. Therefore, the person is usually gradually exposed to types of situations that normally invoke a fearful response while engaging in a type of relaxation at the same time, in order to change the conditioned response. In the case of a fear of penetration (with or without the physical tightness of the pelvic muscles), the client will be progressively and safely exposed to different levels of the phobic stimulus (objects near or penetrating her vagina) in order for her to gradually overcome her anxiety, fear, or disgust associated with these types of activities. One example I often describe to clients is if they were afraid of dogs, it would not be helpful (but instead counterproductive at times) to just put the client in a room with a dog and expect her to be relaxed and be able to pet him. This could actually backfire as her fears might intensify due to being in a highly stressful situation, which may lead to the dog reacting defensively or negatively as well, thus reinforcing her fears. It is much more productive to gradually expose her to pictures, thoughts, and ideas of the dog to begin with, followed by safe encounters with the dog that start from a distance and safely and slowly progress to closer interactions at a pace that works for her. There will naturally be some discomfort and anxiety during the interactions, but the level of anxiety should be bearable and manageable. The key is for the client to sit with the anxiety, learn to soothe herself and relax during, until the anxiety dissipates, before ending the interaction.

The reason I usually begin with a more general exploration of the whole body before the client attempts to use dilators or any other method of genital exploration and desensitization is because for most of my clients, the mere thought of looking at or touching the genitals was too stressful or even impossible for them at the beginning. I therefore felt it would be more productive to begin with less intimidating exercises that safely and gradually build up to ones that focus more on the genitals, and that also help her create a more positive relationship with her body overall. It therefore depends on the level of distress the client is experiencing with sex, penetration, and her genitals when it comes to deciding how "advanced" in the program the client can start off at. Nonetheless, I almost always suggest that the client starts with the non-genital body exploration first as I find that it usually helps build more confidence and comfort with her body. Relating this to the example of a phobia of dogs, if looking at pictures of dogs or talking about dogs is still too distressing for this client, then it may help to take a step back and start with discussing animals that are less intimidating for her in order to build more confidence in her around interacting with animals in general, before moving more specifically into the area of dogs.

What tends to happen when a woman is fearful about PIV sex and yet continues to attempt it without working her way to that stage gradually, is that her fears are maintained due to continuous difficult, painful, and stressful sexual experiences. I think it would be much more effective to support her through learning to manage her anxiety and fears by safely and progressively exposing her to different types and levels of sexual and physical contact that eventually lead to vaginal penetrative sex at a pace that is comfortable for her.

My general recommendation to female clients is to follow each exercise as per the instructions starting with the body image exercise, even if she feels some of the exercises will be easy for her. My suggestion is to <u>practice each step three times a week</u> over at least a week or two, and to not skip any steps. If after one or two weeks the client still feels significantly uncomfortable or distressed during the exercise, then I would suggest she continues practicing the same step two to three times a week until her experience during the exercise shifts to a more comfortable and pleasant one. If the level of her difficulties is mild, then she will probably move forward with the exercises more quickly.

If, however, she is finding some of the exercises difficult, I have found that it has been helpful for me to encourage her to not give up, to trust the process, and to discuss her difficulties with me. From my experience, <u>consistency</u> is one of the most important determinants of treatment success. If she feels she needs to modify the exercise, I encourage her to use her intuition and judgment and be creative with it. For example, if looking at her whole body is difficult to begin with, then she can break it down to smaller chunks and focus on specific parts each time until she can integrate them all and practice the full exercise more easily. If she needs to take a step back and repeat the previous exercise, then it would be more helpful for her to do that a few more times until she is ready to move forward, rather than completely stopping the program altogether.

I have also found that it is common for women to feel uncomfortable or awkward at first, and that usually the more they practice, the easier it gets, until the majority of women eventually learn to enjoy it. It is therefore helpful for most clients to learn that the awkwardness and discomfort they may experience at first is a normal part of the process. Also, from my experience, many women often have a negative view of their bodies at first, but their view tends to shift to a more positive and accepting one with more practice. Additionally, it is quite common for any or all the exercises in this book to initially feel mechanical and boring. Nevertheless, they usually become a more positive and pleasant experience with practice.

A word of caution: some of these exercises might bring up some previous trauma or painful emotions (for example if the client has a very low or negative body image or has been sexually abused or assaulted). In such cases, it is advisable for the client to stop the exercises, especially if she is working through them without the support of a mental health professional, and to seek professional help.

Body Image Exercise

The purpose of this exercise is for you to explore your body through sight to get to know it better. Additionally, this exercise is meant to help you understand how you feel about your body and how your view of your body affects your sexuality.

The exercise itself will take you around 30 minutes. However, I suggest you block off 45–60 minutes so that you can take your time and not feel rushed.

The first part of this practice is experienced in a bath or shower. If you have a bathtub, run yourself a bath, and spend around 10–15 minutes relaxing in it. If you do not have a bathtub, then spend around the same time relaxing in the shower as you feel the warm water running down your body. Though it is not necessary, if you would like to set the bathroom up ahead of time to make it more relaxing by adding some bubbles, candles, and very soft (non-distracting) music, feel free to do so. I would encourage you to view this as a self-care practice and take this opportunity to have some relaxing "me-time" as if you have a spa in your own home.

While you are in the bath or shower, I'd like you to bring your attention to how the water feels on your skin. Be present and focus on the sensations you are experiencing, in addition to how you are feeling during. Then close your eyes and imagine your body in your mind, and notice what feelings and thoughts are coming up for you. Open your eyes and look at your body in the water, and just reflect on how you feel about what you see when you look at all the different parts of your body. Notice whether you like what you see and what parts you would want to change if you could. This is also an opportunity for you to practice any of the breathing or relaxation exercises mentioned previously, especially if you are starting to feel tense or anxious. Relax and finish your bath/shower.

Next, you will need a mirror, preferably full-length if possible. Take your time to dry yourself gently and slowly and, once you are dry, stand in front of the mirror and look at yourself. Ideally this should be done naked, but if you feel uncomfortable being naked then you can keep the towel on. For the next 10–15 minutes, take some time to mindfully look at every part of your body in the mirror (as in Figure 5.2), starting with your head, hair, and face, noticing what comes up for you in your mind as you look. Next, run through your whole body while paying attention to and reflecting on how you are feeling about yourself and what kinds of messages and thoughts you hear as you look at each part. Take some time to

Figure 5.2 Woman looking at herself in the mirror.

look at each part of your body such as your breasts, stomach, arms and shoulders, hips, pubic hair, down to your legs and feet. If you are still uncomfortable taking your towel off, that is OK. Just do what you can and when you are ready the next time you practice this, you may slowly lower your towel until you feel comfortable taking it off fully. Lastly, turn around and look at your back side in the mirror as well. Throughout this whole process, notice what feelings come up for you as you observe each part of your body, specifically regarding how you feel about yourself sexually.

After you have taken the time to thoroughly explore your view of your body, take a few moments to process the experience and write down a summary of how it went, and what you learned from it. Reflect on questions like: Were most of your thoughts critical or positive? Did you feel sexy? Did you feel bored? Did you feel shy or uncomfortable? Overall, how much do you like your body? What did you like the most? What did you like the least? What parts of your body make you feel sexual? What parts of your body would you want to change? What type of body do you think is attractive? Where do you get your views of what an attractive body is from? What are the erotic parts of your body? What parts do you try to hide through what you wear? And what parts do you accentuate with your clothing? How does your view of your body influence your sexuality?

As mentioned previously, many women may feel bored, awkward, neutral, or negative about their bodies at first. The trend that I have observed, however, is that after consistently practicing the body image exercise around three times a week for around two weeks, they start to experience a positive shift in the way they view their bodies. For example, some of them may initially tend to focus more on the imperfections and things they do not like about their bodies, but after practicing it a few times, they start to feel more accepting about their bodies and have less judgmental thoughts, and may even stop noticing the areas they first criticized themselves for.

This is why it is important to keep encouraging the client to continue to practice this exercise even if she is not motivated to do so until she feels more accepting and positive toward her body. As many clients tend to focus on what is *not* working, it is important to remind them of what *is* working or shifting, and to celebrate those achievements, no matter how small they may be. Additionally, recognizing how difficult this process is for the client and allowing her to acknowledge how much courage and persistence she is demonstrating is another piece I find that can be encouraging for the client. I feel it is also helpful to set clear and realistic expectations for the client and explain that feeling positive toward her body does not necessarily have to mean feeling excited or aroused during the exercise, or experiencing pleasure or great enjoyment. The purpose is mainly for the client to develop greater awareness of her feelings toward her body, how these feelings affect her sexual views and feelings, and to start creating a healthier relationship with her body.

If the client has experienced a positive shift toward her body and feels comfortable and more accepting with it, she may then move on to the body exploration section of the Self-Sensate program. Again, the shift need not be transformational to the extent that she thoroughly loves her body or feels joy looking at it, but it needs to be a sufficient degree of acceptance and comfort that she does not experience significant negative emotions or thoughts during.

<u>Body Exploration</u>

Step 1: Mindful Bath

Schedule a time three times a week when you can be on your own with no distractions for around 45 minutes. If you find it difficult to plan this amount of time three times a week, then aim for twice a week and allow yourself some flexibility throughout the week to practice it a third time if possible. Make sure you only continue this Self-Sensate exercise when you feel good. If you feel very stressed and are unable to relax, it may be best to postpone this exercise to another day when you are not feeling worried or pressured. Imagine you are going to a spa to unwind and pamper yourself. Run yourself a bath using your favorite bubbles or oil to relax in. Make sure the bathroom is a comfortable temperature and setting, feel free to light some candles and play some gentle music in the background, and then relax into the bath. If it helps, you can close your eyes and visualize yourself somewhere relaxing, and practice one of the breathing or relaxation exercises that we have covered such as the progressive muscular relaxation or box breathing exercises. Think about your body as something completely new for you to explore. Once again, if you do not have a bathtub, you may modify this, and do what you can in the shower.

When you feel deeply relaxed, shift your focus to your body. Pay attention to how it feels in the water, your physical sensations, your skin, and other parts of your body. Move around in the water, and get a sense of your arms, hands, legs, feet, bottom, back, stomach, breasts, nipples, and your genital area. Try to associate positive thoughts, images, and feelings with this experience, and when you feel ready to end the bath, you may start draining the water. As the water drains away, imagine all your stress and negative thoughts leaving with the water as you stay with only the pleasant feelings that you focused on.

Once you leave the bathtub or shower, wrap yourself in a large, warm towel. Before you start drying yourself, just think for a moment about how you usually do that. Many of us tend to rush the process and use rapid abrupt movements to dry ourselves quickly. For this exercise, I encourage you to slow it down, way down, and use gentle and soft motions to dry your arms first. Notice how it feels to try a slower and softer approach, and then try applying some more pressure or just patting yourself dry and reflect on the difference in the experience and sensations between the various methods. Approach the other parts of your body

80   *Mastering Her Body*

such as your chest, shoulders, stomach, back, and legs in a similar fashion, while paying attention to how it feels. Finally, focus on drying your feet and toes, and your hands and fingers carefully. Once you are done, you may put a robe on or remain naked and reflect on what you learned about yourself and how the experience felt.

Step 2: Body Awareness Through Touch

If Step 1 felt comfortable for you, continue with Step 2 within the same session. Otherwise, please repeat Step 1 two to three times over a week or two until you are completely at ease before moving onto Step 2.

The purpose of Step 2 is to become more aware of and familiar with your body, specifically with regards to touch. Step 2 is done as a follow-up to Step 1, so please begin with Step 1, and after bathing and drying yourself, either sit or lie down and use your favorite oil or lotion and start to apply it on your body (as in Figure 5.3). For this exercise, however, you are to apply it very mindfully, following these guidelines: start with your face and neck (you may use a specific face cream for this part), and gently and slowly apply the cream while avoiding your eyes to be careful not to irritate them. Pay attention to how that feels, which parts of your neck and face do you enjoy being touched on, and what kind of touch feels good. Run your fingers through your hair and touch your scalp and the back of your neck using different strokes to explore what feels best to you.

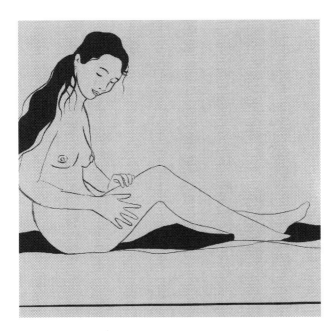

Figure 5.3 Woman exploring her body through touch.

Using a similar approach, move on to your shoulders, arms, hands, and fingers, spending time on each specific part. Experiment with various speeds, pressure, and roughness as you work the cream or oil into your skin. Pay attention to your fingers and nails as well. All throughout this process focus on the feelings and thoughts that come up and reflect on what types of touch and strokes feel pleasant to you.

Next move on to your chest, breasts, and stomach, and take your time as you explore different types of sensations while applying your lotion. Remember to take things slow as you enjoy the touch of your own skin. Let yourself flow as you move down to your thighs, legs, and feet. Many people find the feet to be very pleasurable to touch, so feel free to spend some extra time enjoying that. Applying a firm grip can help you adjust to the touch if you find yourself to be ticklish on your feet or any other part of your body. Make sure to not neglect your toes and to spend some time massaging them. Once you have covered the front side of your body, rub some lotion onto your buttocks and as far as you can onto your back, though it can be challenging to reach all parts of your back. You may want to sit up or even stand for this part. You can try applying the lotion on the back of your hands as you reach as far as you can up your back. Throughout this exercise, make sure to vary the way you touch yourself and notice how you feel with different types of pressure, softness, roughness, and speeds. Think about what feels more pleasant and enjoyable to you, whether it is fast or slow motions, firm or soft grips, rough or gentle touches.

Once you have mindfully applied your lotion or oil all over your body, spend a little time focusing on touching specific parts. Explore different strokes around and under your breasts and touch different parts of your breasts. Go through the skin between your legs, under your arms, and between your buttocks. Notice how heavy, soft, warm, smooth, rough, and firm each part feels. Run your fingers through your pubic hair and notice what comes up for you in terms of sensations and what parts feel good.

It is completely natural if you feel uncomfortable or strange when you first practice this touching exercise. In most cases it tends to become easier with more practice and you will start to feel more comfortable each time. It is advisable that you repeat it two to three times a week until it feels more familiar and comfortable. I always encourage you to trust your intuition and go at a pace that feels best for you, even if that means skipping an area of your body or modifying one of the parts until you feel ready at a later time. It is important to use each practice session as an opportunity to learn about your body and how you like to be touched.

When you feel comfortable enough, spend a little more time gently massaging your breasts and noticing any changes. It is normal for your breasts and nipples to change in response to touch as the breasts tend to become a little firmer and the nipples may become harder and more erect. If you feel ready at this stage, you may lightly explore your genital area without going too deep or into too much detail just yet. Simply run your hands and fingers over your genitals for a few seconds and pay attention to what it feels like in terms of shape, texture, and temperature. Also notice what thoughts and emotions come up as you do this. If you do not feel ready to touch your genital area yet, that is completely OK. You will have more opportunities at a later stage to get more comfortable and explore your genitals gradually and safely.

Each time you finish Step 2, lie or sit down for a few minutes and relax. Reflect on each step of the process and think about what you have learned about yourself, your body, your sensations, your breasts, and your genitals.

End this exercise here, and practice Step 2 three times a week for at least one or two weeks. Do not move on to Step 3 until you have practiced Steps 1 and 2 several times and they feel completely comfortable to you.

Step 3: Body Awareness Through Touch and Sight

Our feelings about our body affect how we feel and act sexually. It is therefore important to be aware of those feelings in order to create a positive shift in our relationship with our sexuality. The purpose of Step 3 is to help you overcome the negative thoughts and feelings you may have about your body. Therefore, in this step, you will become aware of what you like and do not like, and how your preferences may be affecting your sexual feelings.

Step 3 is similar to Step 2, except that you will also need a full-length mirror or one in which you can see most of your body. Firstly, repeat Step 1 to relax. After your bath apply some cream, oil, or lotion as in Step 2, and this time look at yourself in the mirror as you mindfully touch your body. Follow the same guidelines in Step 2 and make sure you are spending time paying attention to the sensation of touching each part of your body, in addition to how you feel as you look at the part you are stroking. Think about what it is you like or dislike about each part. Work down your body as you did in Step 2, watching yourself as you go.

When you have finished, spend some time standing in front of the mirror, focusing on what you see, and thinking about what you like about each part and what emotions and thoughts come up for you. Go through every part starting at the top of your head, your hair, each part of your face, your neck, and your skin. Then move on to your shoulders, arms, hands, fingers, breasts, belly, hips, and pubic hair, as you continue along to your legs, feet, and toes. Reflect on how you like about the different shapes, sizes, colors, and textures of what you see. Turn around and look at your back and bottom, or use a hand mirror if needed.

After you have finished, lie down, relax, and take a few moments to think about what this experience was like for you. I encourage you to write in your journal as much detail as you can remember about what you have seen and how you felt during the exercise. Repeat this exercise at least twice more over the next week or two, until it feels easier and more comfortable.

Step 4: Genital Exploration

You can practice this exercise on its own, but initially you will probably feel more relaxed if you repeat Steps 1 to 3 or some variation of them first. As in previous steps, only move on to Step 4 if you have been able to practice Step 3 a few times and have completed it comfortably. You will need a small mirror for this exercise, preferably one that can stand on its own. Lie on the bed and relax. Practice the box breathing or the progressive muscular relaxation exercise for a few minutes until you feel completely relaxed.

Once you have relaxed and feel ready, sit up and lean against the headboard of your bed. You can use extra pillows if you need more support. Open your legs and place the mirror on the bed in front of you where you can comfortably see your genital area. If you feel unable to continue, stop now, and try again another day. Don't worry: even if you just take a quick glance and stop, it will feel less strange each time you look. Try to remember another time in your life where you were initially uncomfortable with a new style or look or were even disgusted with looking at a certain image or even a food. It probably took you a few attempts or days to get accustomed to it and maybe even enjoy it eventually. You may use the illustration provided in Figure 5.4 as a guideline to identify the main parts of your genital area. Please keep in mind, however, that every woman's genitals look different, just as our faces and bodies differ, so don't worry if you don't look exactly like the drawing provided.

Let's start with your mons pubis and pubic hair. The mons pubis (which is also specifically known in females as the mons veneris) is the fatty tissue lying over your pubic bone, which is covered by pubic hair. The mons pubis mainly serves as a cushioning during sexual intercourse, and your pubic hair serves as a protection for this sensitive area of your body from irritation by external factors or perspiration. Look at your pubic hair and notice what color it is. Is it straight or curly, long or short? Which parts of your genital area have more pubic hair than others? How do you feel about the color, texture, and amount of your pubic hair? Run your fingers through and think about how that feels.

Next, take a look at your vaginal lips (labia), which comprise the inner and outer lips. The outer lips (labia majora) and inner lips (labia minora) vary in shape and size, and while for the majority of women the inner lips are smaller, this may not be the case for everyone. For some women, one side has larger or longer lips than the other. And sometimes the labia minora hang down between the labia majora, which can make them visible when looking at yourself in the mirror while standing. Again, variations in shapes, sizes, and colors are completely normal. If you are comfortable, hold the labia majora with your fingers

84 *Mastering Her Body*

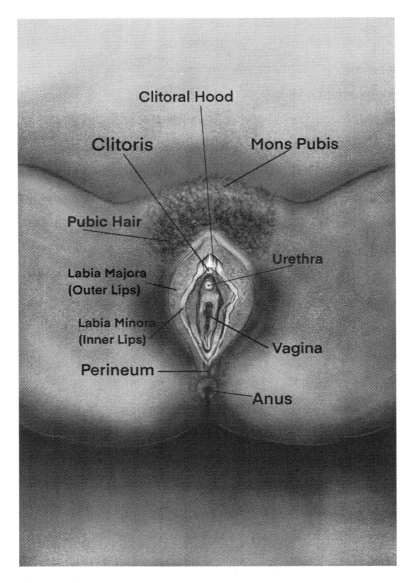

Figure 5.4 Vulva anatomy.

and gently pull them apart to be able to see the labia minora more clearly. Pay attention to the colors, shapes, and textures. The color of women's labia generally tends to vary from shades of pink to different shades of brown. The next illustration in Figure 5.5 shows examples of various shapes and sizes of female genitals.

Mastering Her Body 85

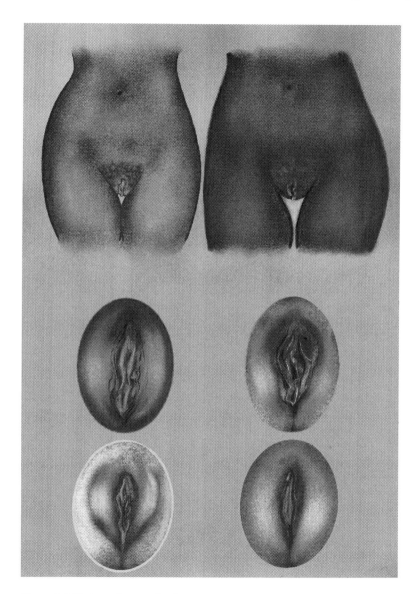

Figure 5.5 Various shapes of vulvas.

Now turn your attention slightly above to the clitoral hood. This is usually where the labia minora meet, but not always. The clitoral hood is similar to the foreskin on a penis; it is a fold of skin that protects the clitoris. Gently pull the clitoral hood back to reveal the clitoris itself, which is a small round gland under the clitoral hood. In some women, the clitoral hood cannot be pulled back much, which does not tend to be related to sexual functioning, and surgical procedures to detach the hood are not necessary. The clitoris is highly sensitive to touch. In the past it was thought that the vagina was responsible for female sexual pleasure, and although the vagina, and indeed the whole body, is involved in sexual stimulation, it is the clitoris that plays the most important role in sexual sensations and pleasure in women.

Next, take a look a little south of the clitoris and you will notice the opening of the urethra above the vaginal opening. The urethral opening is where the urine passes. Just below the urethra you will find the opening of the vagina. Take a look at its shape, size, colors, and texture. The vagina is the elastic muscular passage or canal inside that connects the external genitals to the uterus. Though we often refer to the vaginal opening as the vagina, technically the vagina is internal. The term "vulva" (which is the female external sex organs) more accurately represents what we mean when we say "vagina," and that includes the labia, vaginal opening, clitoris, and the urethral opening. The anatomical diagram of the female genitals above illustrates the vulva. Moving further down and back you will find the anus, which is the opening through which stool leaves the body. The area between the vagina and the anus is called the perineum. Some women and men find the stimulation of the perineum to be quite pleasurable. Try to do some Kegel exercises and contract and relax your pelvic muscles (imagine you are urinating and then you need to pause your urine, this is a contraction, and then you want to let go and continue urinating, this is relaxed), you should be able to see some movement of your vaginal opening or the muscles around when you do this.

Once you have visually explored all the different parts, take a few minutes to relax and breathe deeply. Notice any feelings or thoughts that you are left with after having completed this exercise and write down some reflections on what you felt as you were looking at your genitals, what you liked and disliked, what you may have been surprised about, and what you learned about your body and your feelings about your genitals. Similarly to all the exercises so far, I recommend that you practice this at least two to three times (over a period of a week or two) until you feel more comfortable with looking at your genitals.

It is common for women, especially those who have not explored their sexual organs, to initially feel awkward, or even sometimes disgusted by their genitals. My professional experience has shown me so far that usually their views and feelings toward their genitals shift to a more accepting and potentially even more positive one after getting more accustomed to looking at their vulvas and learning to think about their genitals differently (as discussed on page 36–38).

Step 5: Genital Awareness Through Touch

After feeling more comfortable with Step 4, and if you are ready, you can move on to exploring your genital area through touch. As always, start with one of the breathing or relaxation exercises, and get yourself more prepared for this step by

Mastering Her Body 87

practicing any or all of the Self-Sensate stages (1–4). Spend some time feeling each part carefully. You may do this with or without a mirror, and if you choose to start this practice without a mirror, I would encourage you to work up to practicing it while looking at your genitals in the mirror (as shown in Figure 5.6). Feel each part with your hand and fingers and pay attention to which areas are more sensitive to your touch. Tune in to how the sensations of your fingers feel, and what thoughts or emotions come up as you explore your genitals. You may notice that you are becoming aroused, which is a completely natural response of your body to your touch. If so, you may find that your labia are changing color and becoming larger in size. Your clitoris may also respond and become hard as it disappears under the clitoral hood. Next, pay attention to how your vaginal opening feels, you may notice that it has become moist. And if you do not get aroused, that is also fine. If exploring your genitals through touch feels too difficult for you at this stage, you may start by simply placing your hand over your genital area for a few

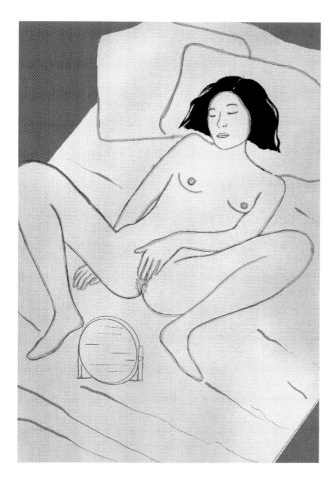

Figure 5.6 Woman exploring her vulva.

minutes until you relax into it. Gradually exposing your genital area to gentle and safe touch will eventually decrease the anxiety and allow it to get accustomed to touch and feel more comfortable with it.

Once you have ended the exercise just sit or lie down for a few minutes and relax as you tune in to any feelings you might have about having done this exercise. Reflect on what you did and allow yourself to be aware of how you felt, what you thought, what you discovered, and what did and did not feel good. The more you repeat this exercise, the more familiar you become with your intimate parts of your body. The majority of women who have practiced the exercises several times tend to feel better about their sexual areas over time. If you find yourself unable to complete the exercise, do not beat yourself up about that. It is important for you to tune in to yourself and trust that you will know how much further you can go. It generally takes a few sessions to feel comfortable with the exercise so just go as far as you can and try to go a little further each time you practice until you carry out the exercises until the end. I find that the woman needs to find that sweet spot of being able to push through a level of discomfort that is tolerable but not damaging or traumatizing, while having faith that she will be able to overcome the challenge and move on to more specific sexual exercises soon.

For those of you whose religious or cultural beliefs may impede your genital exploration, I would gently remind you that this is not a form of masturbation. Masturbation has the purpose of producing pleasure and ultimately orgasm, whereas this is merely an exercise to understand your body better, with no intent of pleasuring yourself. Just like you would be expected to examine your breasts for any lumps every month, you can approach this from a medical perspective and consider it as part of your treatment (which it is), and not masturbation.

Though masturbation is a normal and healthy part of men and women's sexuality, it is up to you if you would like to take the exercise further and explore what pleasures you. If you choose not to, that is OK, just practice getting more familiar and comfortable with your genital area through touch without pleasure. Even if the exercise feels mechanical, it is important that you get familiar with your anatomy, so that you can feel more in control of your own body. Please note, however, that if you feel any pain or soreness during this exploration, I would recommend that you see a medical doctor, just to make sure there is nothing medically amiss.

Typically, in my work with a client, we discuss in our sessions how each of the Self-Sensate exercises went. Every week we would meet and follow up on her progress and challenges with each step. Often the client feels uncomfortable with the idea of doing the exercises, and may even at times believe it will be impossible for her to reach a place where she can look at or touch her genital area. I found that it is helpful to focus on what she *can* do at the moment, to provide encouragement, and to give her permission to take it at a pace that feels right for her. Part of the therapeutic process also involves, of course, addressing her discomfort with the exercise and identifying where that discomfort comes from, in addition to working on new ways to reframe her thoughts and views on exploring her body.

Some clients may only need to practice each step two to three times and are able to move comfortably to the next step more quickly than others. Nonetheless, I still want to make sure that the client's experience during each exercise has shifted so that she is ready for the next one before moving on. She does not necessarily need to be enjoying the exercise or feel pleasant or pleasurable sensations or emotions, but she needs to have overcome the intense discomfort, awkwardness, anxiety, and disgust she may have experienced in the beginning.

Solo Genital Exposure Progressions

Once the client feels more comfortable with and accepting of her body and genitals, and has learned how to be more mindful of her experience and sensations in the moment, we then focus on her gradually exposing her vaginal area to different levels of penetration. As mentioned previously, the idea behind these progressions is for the client to safely experience different levels of touch and penetration in her vagina while working through her anxiety until she reaches a more relaxed state, so that her brain and body unlearn previous conditioned responses, and form new safe and positive connections. The exercises described next are based on what I would generally verbally discuss with the client in sessions, which means that it is usually a less structured and more fluid process depending on the client's needs. Therefore, I would encourage the clinician and reader to use them as a general guideline and to feel free to modify them when appropriate.

Finger-On-Vulva Contact

Now that you feel more comfortable with your body and genital area, it is time to start gradually experiencing what penetration feels like by training your vagina and progressively inserting your finger(s). Other practitioners and books recommend using dilators for the desensitization, which works for many women and can be used here if that is more comfortable for you. However, I encourage you to use your fingers because they are more real, you can feel your body on the inside, you have more control over the angle and movements, and you don't have to worry about finding dilators if they are not accessible to you. One thing to keep in mind while working through the following progressions is that these exercises are not intended to lead to pleasure, and so while some women may feel pleasurable sensations, it is also completely OK if you do not feel pleasure or sexual feelings during. It is common for women to find these exercises mechanical, so don't lose hope if you are not necessarily enjoying them.

Almost every woman I have worked with who had not been in therapy for their sexual difficulty before has never explored her genital area by touch, and the first reaction I get when I explain the genital work that they are about to embark on is that of shock and disgust. They do not believe they will ever get to a stage where they can insert their own finger, and it actually feels completely alien and disgusting to them. I can say with great certainty that the great majority of the women I worked with who have committed to the process, despite it being challenging and them thinking they will never get there, have eventually managed to insert their finger and felt less disgusted and uncomfortable with it, and in time, most learn to feel at ease and comfortable with this part of their body. Every woman's journey is different, and some will take longer than others and might need to take a step back at times, but they have all gotten there with patience, commitment, and consistency.

The first step in the progressive genital exposure part of the Self-Sensate program is to practice Steps 1 and 2 again (on pages 79–80), then gradually touch parts of your genital area for a few moments to acclimate it and get more comfortable. You may follow the guidelines of Step 5 (page 86) to help your body get accustomed and relaxed if you still feel tense and your genital area is still not prepared. Once you feel ready, start gently placing the tip of your forefinger on the outside of your vaginal opening as illustrated in Figure 5.7. Do not attempt to insert your finger just yet, simply keep the tip of your finger on the outside of the vaginal opening for a few moments until your anxiety or discomfort subsides. I urge you again to listen to your intuition and always modify each exercise according to your needs. For this step and the remainder of the genital progressions, feel free to use a hand mirror to look at what you are doing and be able to control your hand and finger movements better. If you prefer not to use a mirror, that is also OK.

You might feel like you want to immediately remove your finger as soon as you get uncomfortable, but it is very important that you DO NOT immediately stop and withdraw your finger simply because it feels challenging. Of course, if you feel pain, or if it is triggering an unbearable emotional reaction or severe distress, please stop immediately. If the level of discomfort is bearable, just sit with it for a few moments, practice some deep breathing such as the box breathing or the progressive muscular relaxation exercise mentioned previously, and when you feel more relaxed and your anxiety has mostly dissipated, you may stop the exercise and remove your finger. This is the approach I would recommend the client adopts for the remainder of the genital exposure progressions.

The reason we want to go through the discomfort and only remove your finger after you have relaxed is because this is helping to condition your brain and body that nothing dangerous or painful is going to happen. The more frequently your genitals are exposed to safe interactions and touch, the easier it will become to relax. This way the conditioned fearful response will become extinct, and instead, your brain will associate penetration with a neutral or safe feeling. Withdrawing the finger too soon may prevent the brain from having the opportunity to unlearn the fear as the avoidance will just maintain the anxiety. Practice this step two to three times a week until having the tip of your finger on the outside of your vagina becomes easier and you are ready to take it a bit further.

Mastering Her Body 91

Figure 5.7 Woman placing her finger on her vaginal opening.

Inserting One Finger

Once you feel up for the next level, repeat the same steps, but this time, try to insert just the tip of your forefinger inside your vaginal opening, even if all you can do at this point is just a quarter of the tip of your finger. While you are attempting to insert your finger(s), you may use a lubricant to allow for a smoother process (if you are not moist). Do not attempt to go deeper just yet, but once again, just keep the tip of your finger inside for a few moments, breathing deeply, until you relax into it. If you feel this is too difficult, then go back to the step before and practice that a few more times. Come back to this step after you feel you have mastered the last one. Practice this step two to three times a week as well until it feels more achievable and comfortable, even if it takes you several weeks.

Alternative suggestion: If the forefinger seems too difficult for you, try your pinky instead. Though the angle might be more awkward, the fact that it is smaller might make it more feasible for you at this point. If you are able to work with your pinky instead of your forefinger for the remainder of the steps, feel free to do that until you build enough confidence and comfort to practice the exercises again with your forefinger.

Throughout the genital progressions, play around with the Kegel exercises if you feel your vaginal muscles are tight. Remember to contract and relax your pelvic muscles so that you can control them and intentionally relax them when you need to insert your finger. If your vaginal opening seems tense, practice your Kegel exercises a few times while breathing deeply and try to insert your finger when you consciously relax your pelvic muscles.

After having mastered the last step, next time try to go a little bit further with your finger (continue to use lubricant if needed). Do not go too deep yet, just go as far as you feel is enough for you at this point. This may look like a third of your finger, or more, depending on how far you can go. Remember that there is no failing, so don't set any specific expectations throughout this process, just do as much as you can while trying to go a little bit further each time. It will not always be consistent, so even if you were able to go deeper one time, it does not mean that it will happen every time. You might have to keep practicing until it becomes easier and more consistent, or even go back to a previous step again for a couple of times. Similarly to previous steps, keep your finger in for a few moments while practicing one of the breathing/relaxation exercises until your anxiety dissipates and you relax into it before you remove it.

Keep trying to progressively go a bit further each time you practice until you are able to insert your whole finger. Most women think this is impossible when they first begin therapy – they cannot even imagine it would ever happen. However, with consistency and going at the right pace for you, you can and will do it. And when you do, it will create a significant shift in your perspective as you will have experienced something you never thought you could. This will tremendously build your confidence.

One key point to remember though is that you should keep these exercises light and positive. Sure, they might be uncomfortable, but they should not be painful (if they are, you should stop immediately and go back to the previous step or seek professional help), and they should not be too stressful. What I mean by too stressful is you should not be spending hours each day forcing yourself to progress, feeling very frustrated and disappointed – this will be counterproductive as it will only reinforce negative experiences with your body and genital area. Know your limits and the level of discomfort that is safe for you to engage in. If you continue to struggle with attempting to insert your finger, I would advise you to consult a qualified sex therapist or pelvic floor physical therapist.

Case Example

Iman is a 22 year-old woman from Pakistan who had been married for around ten months. She had no sexual experience whatsoever before marriage, and very minimal education and knowledge about sexuality and the genitals. Her husband is a very patient and gentle man who also had no sexual experience prior to their marriage and basic knowledge about sex. They had attempted vaginal intercourse several times throughout the months after marriage and have not been finding it easier with time. She appeared to be quite anxious and impatient about getting immediate results in therapy, even when she was progressing through her solo exercises. When she struggled with an exercise, she expressed significant distress and disappointment, which emphasized to me the importance of her learning patience and working on letting go and trusting the process. It is quite easy to collude with a client in these situations and feel anxious ourselves and panic about not getting results "quickly," and yet I feel it could be more damaging to try to speed things up, especially in situations like this. Trying to rush the exercises and progress could set her up for even more pressure and disappointment. Therefore I, as the therapist, needed to keep myself grounded and work with her through some of her unrealistic expectations and her emotional blocks during the exercises before moving to the next progressions. It was extremely helpful for her to acknowledge her feelings, validate the difficulties she was experiencing, and at the same time remind her to trust herself and stay consistent. She soon after was able to get through all of the genital progressions and gained a lot of confidence.

When a client manages to insert her finger, and for each small victory throughout the journey for that matter, I feel it is important to celebrate them all. I saw that the achievement of being able to fully insert a finger usually instilled a lot of optimism and confidence in the clients, and gave them tremendous hope and motivation to move forward. But before the client moves on to trying to insert two fingers, I usually encourage her to continue practicing inserting one finger until it feels much easier and is more consistently successful. It might still feel difficult at times despite her having succeeded once or twice, and she might even have trouble inserting it again, but it is important to support her through not getting discouraged. It happens. My job is often to help her keep the focus on the fact that she was able to insert her finger despite once thinking she never would, and to build on that experience to bring her strength and faith to keep going. I also always remind her that she can go back to the previous step if she feels stuck.

Many clients tend to focus on looking forward, and feel frustrated and hopeless when they think of how much more they need to overcome. I noticed that this way of thinking can be very destructive, and tends to put the client down and limit her capacity. I found that the best way to move forward is to focus on the now. Throughout the treatment journey I often work on helping the client learn to shift her focus to the present and think about where she is now and how that compares to where she was a month, two months, or six months ago. Most of the time she will find that so many things have changed in her relationship with her body in ways that surprised her, and knowing that helps motivate her to keep going. This reminds me of when I am exercising, running, or hiking a mountain. As soon as I start thinking of how much longer I have to complete the exercise, or how many more miles I have to finish it or reach the top, I get consumed by frustration, hopelessness, and I feel bored, tired, and lose motivation. However, once I shift my experience back to focusing on each step, on the present moment, and on appreciating what I am doing right now, before I know it I achieve what I want and am more likely to have enjoyed the process.

Inserting Two Fingers

Once you have been successfully inserting your forefinger consistently and easily, take it to the next step and begin the same process of gradually inserting both your forefinger with your middle finger together (using lubricant again if you are not wet enough). Remember to always follow the progressive approach of just inserting the tips first, followed by going a bit further each time (as far as you are comfortable with, and at a pace that is somewhat challenging but not too stressful). Another approach that might work better for some people is to insert one finger first (your forefinger since you have already mastered that), and then insert the tip of your middle finger. Next time you can try to go a little deeper with your middle finger after having fully inserted your forefinger. Practice each stage several times to build confidence before you attempt to go further. Go on with that direction until you are able to insert both fingers fully. The goal is to be able to insert both fingers fully and comfortably. I have seen or heard some resources and experts advise that the goal is to insert three fingers, but from my experience, most women I worked with were able to overcome their fears after they have comfortably inserted two fingers (and sometimes even just one). Therefore, unless deemed necessary for a particular client, consistently inserting two fingers marks the completion of the solo genital exposure progressions.

There are several reasons why completing the individual part of the program is important. Firstly, getting comfortable with your body and touch is necessary for you to be able to be intimate with your partner. And so, practicing it while you are in control of the pace and approach is a safe and effective way to do it. Experiencing a form of penetration will also help you overcome the fear of pain or the unknown as you will realize that it is not painful or scary to insert an object into your vagina.

Secondly, when you understand your body better, you gain more insight into what pleasures you, what feels good, and what doesn't, so that you can guide your partner and have a fulfilling sexual experience. Being properly stimulated is obviously very important in sexual pleasure, and it is your responsibility to know your body and collaborate with your partner on achieving pleasure. Thirdly, the more you familiarize yourself with your body and expose yourself to it in a kind and positive way, the healthier your body image will become. And lastly, the Self-Sensate exercises emphasize practicing how to focus on your sensations, thoughts, and feelings – in other words, to be more mindful of your experience as opposed to being goal-oriented or experiencing performance anxiety.

Some of you may feel ready to attempt PIV sex once you have successfully inserted two fingers, or even just one finger, and for some women, reaching this stage is enough to resolve their fears and consummate their marriage. You have to be the judge of that. However, my recommendation would be to read the whole book even if you successfully complete vaginal penetrative sex, as some concepts are extremely useful to get you mentally and emotionally more prepared, avoid relapsing, and have a more fulfilling and connected intimate life.

If, however, you still choose to attempt vaginal penetrative sex at this point, I would strongly advise that you take on a progressive approach similar to the one we have been following in this book so far. Do not go straight into attempting vaginal intercourse all the way. Instead, make sure that you get enough sensual touch and arousal, and that you warm up your genital area with your fingers. It is encouraged that you build sufficient sexual arousal, feel sexually excited and relaxed, and are lubricated enough to aid with the penetration. I would also suggest that you take the lead and choose a position you feel most comfortable and safe in, and guide your partner's penis toward your vaginal opening and take gradual steps in inserting it. You may even need to do this over several sessions before you are able to have full PIV sex.

6 Incorporating the Partner

Once the client has completed all of the solo exercises, she may then proceed to the couple's part of the sensate exercises – Sensate Focus (described in this chapter). I generally only start this stage if the client feels comfortable and ready to touch and be touched by her partner. I reassure her that it is still going to be a gradual approach that starts with no genital or sexual touching and progresses to more intimate touching. Usually, I recommend that the client follow this program under the supervision of a professional who is familiar with and trained in Sensate Focus, in case it brings up more complex issues. When working with a client or couple through the Sensate Focus program, we would process how the experience was for them during our sessions and discuss any potential modifications before moving forward. However, if the client is to be following this program on her own, she must stop and consult a trained therapist if at any point it feels too uncomfortable or triggers any trauma or more intense feelings.

Some women may feel ready to attempt penetration with their partner after completing the Self-Sensate and solo genital exposure program and may skip the Sensate Focus section. This decision is up to the practitioner and client as each case is different depending on her comfort level and the severity of the issue to begin with. Some women will have success by moving on to the partner-assisted genital exposure (page 107) and then attempting PIV sex without going through the Sensate Focus program, while some women might think they are ready when in reality their body still is not. One of the main factors that I believe should be considered in this situation is the level of arousal that the woman experiences with her partner. If she is sufficiently aroused, relaxed, and lubricated with her partner, and she is able to enjoy sensual and intimate touch, then she may not need to go through the Sensate Focus portion of the treatment. If she is not aroused, lubricated, or comfortable with her partner's intimate touch, then I highly recommend that they go through the Sensate Focus program together to build the sensual and intimate connection, comfort, and sexual arousal. Regardless of the situation, I still believe that the Sensate Focus program would be beneficial to all, when they are ready for it, and is a great tool for couples to reduce the anxiety associated with sex and create a more pleasurable experience.

Sensate Focus Overview and Purpose

Most of us are taught or believe that good sex means being able to turn your partner on, and for our partner to be able to turn us on, and that watching certain movies or reading certain magazines is supposed to teach us how to do that. There is also often too much of a focus on the performance and the outcome (i.e., orgasm) as measures of "good sex." In reality, the way sex works and happens naturally is by really tuning into our own sensations, to be present in the moment, without expectations of a specific outcome. Sensate Focus is a program that teaches people to do that. William Master and Virginia Johnson, who were pioneers in the sex therapy field, developed Sensate Focus, which is defined below, for resolving sexual difficulties and improving intimacy (Weiner & Avery-Clark, 2017, p. 8).

> Sensate Focus is a series of structured touching and discovery suggestions that provides opportunities for experiencing your own and your partner's bodies in a non-demand, exploratory way without having to read each other's minds. Non-demand exploration is defined as touching for your own interest without regard for trying to make sexual response, pleasure, enjoyment or relaxation happen for yourself or your partner, or prevent them from happening. Touching for your own interest is further defined as focusing on the touch sensations of temperature, pressure, and texture. Temperature, pressure, and texture are even more specifically defined as cool or warm, hard or soft (firm or light), and smooth or rough.
>
> (Weiner & Avery-Clark, 2017, p. 8)

There are several purposes behind Sensate Focus that are usually helpful to explain to clients to help them understand why they are doing what they are doing. Some of these objectives are general to most sexual difficulties, and some are specific to working with GPPPD (the list below is based on the book: *A Clinician's Guide to Systemic Sex Therapy*, by Weeks, Gambescia, & Hertlein, 2016, pp. 156–163).

1 **To reduce anxiety associated with sex:** The foundation of Sensate Focus is based on the concept of systematic desensitization, which is a gradual exposure to situations that make the clients anxious in order to help them overcome the anxiety and negative associations with those situations. It is a similar concept to the solo genital exposure progressions in which the client creates new neutral or positive associations with situations that used to create anxiety. Therefore, the couple goes through exercises together to help them reduce the discomfort or anxiety with intimacy, and then move on to more difficult progressions once that anxiety has been reduced. For the woman with huge fears of penetration or pain, allowing her to experience gradual and safe progressions of physical and intimate touch with her partner can help replace the fear associated with sex with neutral or positive feelings.

2. **To help interrupt the cycle of avoidance:** As mentioned previously, couples who experience sexual difficulties, such as GPPPD, tend to end up avoiding all sexual contact and affection. Therefore, by guiding the couple through incremental, less intense, and safer intimate interactions, it gives them the opportunity to break the cycle of avoidance and incorporate some physical interaction.
3. **To help the clients gain more awareness of their own sensations:** When people are consumed with anxiety or self-evaluation during sex, it becomes more difficult for them to focus on the experience and pleasurable sensations. By learning to shift their attention to the physical sensations, it helps them explore and understand their own feelings of touch without worrying about their performance or partner's feelings.
4. **To help the clients focus more on their own needs for pleasure and worry less about the problem or the partner:** This is related to the previous point, with the addition of learning to enjoy their sensual and sexual touch. Often the clients are preoccupied with the problem or with the fear of disappointing their partner. One of the goals is to allow themselves to focus on what each of them needs to feel more sensation and pleasure.
5. **To learn how to communicate about their sensual and sexual needs and desires:** Many couples, especially those who hold more shame and anxiety around sex, feel uncomfortable expressing their sexual needs and wants. Through learning to be more self-aware and creating a safe and progressive approach, the couple gradually verbalizes and communicates with each other how they feel about the touch and what they want.
6. **To increase awareness of the partner's sexual and sensual needs/ desires:** One of the common sexual myths is that one should know what the partner wants without communicating it, as if we are told we should be able to read each other's minds or that there is a specific way to pleasure men or women that we should know. This unrealistic belief can lead to a lot of anxiety, anger, frustration, disappointment, and to feeling unloved if one believes that truly loving someone means knowing what they desire. Though people often think their partner does not care about them because they do not know what they desire, in reality, they probably haven't clearly communicated what they really wanted. And so though Sensate Focus aims to teach clients to focus on their own sensations and desires, they are also encouraged to ask for what they want and notice or ask about their partner's wants and feelings.
7. **To broaden the couple's view of sexuality and intimate touch:** Often in long-term relationships sexual behaviors become quite repetitive and routine, with a lot of focus on the performance or orgasm. By encouraging the clients to be creative and explore different ways to touch and feel pleasure, they expand their repertoire of sensual behaviors and learn to experiment and allow themselves to be open to new activities.

8 **To learn to focus on the experience rather than the outcome:** It is common for couples, especially those with sexual problems, to think of foreplay as a means to an end rather than to appreciate it as an experience of sexual expression in and of itself. Sex becomes less sensual and more focused on the performance. What also ends up happening a lot of the times is that sex becomes transactional where men show affection in order to get sex, and women have sex to get affection. By banning intercourse and other forms of sexual expression that are not part of the exercise, Sensate Focus helps couples appreciate non-penetrative sex and non-sexual pleasure again, without the pressure of it leading to vaginal intercourse.

9 **To nurture more positive interactions and experiences:** Couples with sexual difficulties clearly experience negative outcomes and effects with many of their encounters. The Sensate Focus exercises, if well designed and well timed, help create positive relational experiences and interactions, which help the couple feel like they are moving in the right direction and promote a good feeling about the relationship.

10 **To foster sexual desire:** Desire in the relationship tends to diminish after experiencing sexual difficulties and negative interactions for a period of time. By allowing the couple to shift the focus from their performance or response anxieties (anxiety about not feeling the "correct" feeling) to the enjoyment and sensuality of the touch itself, they start to build more positive rewards, arousal, enthusiasm, and anticipation for physical contact. Sensate Focus can be one of the interventions used to help couples reduce anxiety and reconnect and improve their desire/interest and sexual arousal.

11 **To strengthen the commitment, love, cooperation, and sexual interest in the relationship:** Committing to the Sensate Focus program shows how the couple is prioritizing the relationship, despite them feeling pessimistic in the beginning. Additionally, it is not uncommon for couples to enter therapy feeling that the problem lies within one of the partners. Going through the exercises not only requires a large degree of cooperation between the two, but also helps the couple see how the relationship may have contributed to the problem, thus allowing each of them to take responsibility for their part. At times one partner may be resistant or reluctant with regards to the exercises, and so part of the therapy may be to help them explore whether or not that reflects a lack of commitment to the relationship. Just like I encourage therapists to celebrate and validate even the smallest of victories in the solo exercises, it is also important for the therapist to praise and validate the couples' hard work, commitment, love, care, and progress when the treatment is going well.

This list describes some of the most notable and common benefits and goals of Sensate Focus. Nonetheless, different clients may experience it differently, and of course it is very important to assess whether or not the couple is ready for it. I usually start the program when I sense, through various questions and discussions, that the couple is ready for touching and being touched by their partner, and have a mostly positive attitude about the exercise. I would describe the general overview of the Sensate Focus exercises and specifically the first stage to my clients and notice how each partner reacts, and explore different questions about what it means to them to be sensual, how they feel about physical touch, and how they feel about communicating about touch and their sexual needs. Of course, I also acknowledge and remind them that it is going to be a gradual and structured process, so that they feel they will be going through it in a safe way and know that they are not expected to be completely comfortable with all of that from the beginning. I have found that it was quite common for clients to initially feel awkward and uncomfortable with the idea of the exercise, and so it is important to process these feelings first before they begin. This does not mean that each stage of the program is going to be pleasurable or exciting, in fact, it is quite common for the exercises to feel awkward or boring at first, but they still need to have a sufficient level of readiness and motivation for them to engage in such experiences together.

Sensate Focus Program

The Sensate Focus program described here is partly based on the wonderful book cited earlier that clearly explains and illustrates what Sensate Focus is – *Sensate Focus in Sex Therapy: The Illustrated Manual* by Weiner and Avery-Clark (2017) – and partly based on the way I would verbally describe the exercises to my clients in sessions, and so can be used as a general guideline. As always, however, each stage is adapted according to each client's needs and circumstances, and so I would encourage the clinician and reader to use the program in a way that feels most aligned with the specific client.

> *Stage 1*
>
> *Before you start the exercise, there are some preliminaries that you will need to prepare for in order for you and your partner to have as little distractions and feel as comfortable and as safe as possible during your touching sessions.*
>
> *The exercise is to be done somewhere private, quiet, and comfortable as you will both be spending time naked (most likely), with some soft lighting (you may use lamps if the ceiling light is too bright or uncomfortable). The bedroom is usually the preferred setting, but if it is associated with stress or conflict then it might be better to choose another room. Also, make sure that the room temperature is suitable so that you are not too cold or hot. You may want to lock the door if that is appropriate, to limit potential intrusions if there are other people at home. Remove all possible distractions, such as phones, televisions, and pets.*

Please keep in mind that this experience does not have to feel romantic or relaxing, and so make sure you are not placing any pressure on yourself to create a romantic or enjoyable setting by thinking you have to set candles or music. It is mainly meant to feel comfortable and safe. You may just need a clock somewhere visible so that you can keep track of time, without focusing too much on the clock. You may both want to take a bath or shower first, so that you feel good and fresh.

You are encouraged to set aside a good chunk of unpressured time for the touching sessions when you do not need to rush, you can spend some time reflecting on the session afterwards, and you are not expecting any visitors. You want to choose a time when you are both alert, so not right before going to bed or after a large meal, and when you are not too tired, stressed, hungry, or angry because you just had an argument. I usually suggest setting aside 45 minutes up to an hour for each session so that you do not have to worry about finishing up quickly and have time to process or talk afterwards, although the actual touching will not take an hour.

The aim is to have a touching session three times a week, and to spontaneously decide to do it. However, if you find that you are not getting a session done every two to three days simply by spontaneously starting it, then it may be better to schedule the touching sessions ahead of time. For example, you might either decide together at the beginning of the week on the days and times that work for both of you, or decide on the morning of the day what time works best for both of you that day. Once the first person initiates the first time (spontaneous or not), the initiator must alternate thereafter. Though you are encouraged to both be naked during, if that is too challenging for one or both of you at this time, you may start with a nightgown or underwear, and aim to gradually get more comfortable with removing your clothing and being naked in later sessions.

You will take turns to be the "toucher" and the "touchee" for 10–15 minutes each. The toucher will keep track of time, but make sure you are not too focused on constantly checking the time. You can choose together who starts being the touchee, but make sure to alternate the next time. The first person to be touched lies down naked on their back and relaxes. The toucher (who is also naked), kneels or sits beside the touchee (see Figure 6.1) and begins by caressing and stroking them from head to toe for 5–8 minutes on the front side, while <u>avoiding the genital and sexual areas</u> (breasts, chest, genital area, bottom, and anything else the person considers sexual). You are not allowed to touch each other's sexual areas at this stage yet. Make sure to pay attention to every other part of the touchee's body including the face, earlobes, neck, and toes. After one side has been caressed for 5–8 minutes, the touchee turns over and the toucher takes 5–8 minutes again to stroke the back side. The toucher and the touchee can change positions if they feel more comfortable (for example, standing instead of kneeling beside the touchee, lying side by side, etc.).

It is more important that the time you spend touching is mindful and focused even if it is shorter as opposed to aiming for longer periods of touching that are more distracted. Once you have completed 10–15 minutes in total of touching your partner, swap roles so that the toucher becomes the person who lies down to be touched.

Please note that this exercise is very different from giving someone a massage. In a massage, the person touching is doing so with the intent to pleasure or relax the other person or provide manual therapy. In Sensate Focus, the toucher decides how he/she wants to touch their partner based on what he/she is interested in and with the intent to explore and focus on the sensations. It is therefore for the benefit of the toucher, not for the benefit of the touchee like in a massage. They should vary their technique by using different movements and directions, long and short strokes, different parts of their hands (only hands), different speeds, and different firmness. While the toucher is focusing on the sensations of the touch on his/her skin, hands, and fingers as they touch the partner, the touchee is also paying attention to how the sensations of being touched feel on the different parts of their body.

One of the most important learning outcomes Sensate Focus is designed for is to practice being mindful. In other words, remember to bring your focus back to the experience and really pay attention to your physical sensations when you get distracted. It is impossible for our minds to stay focused on one thing for long periods of time, and so your mind may be jumping from one thought to another. Just be aware of what thoughts come to mind and notice any emotions that come up during the touching sessions, but do not stay in your thoughts or focus too much on your emotions. Instead, gently make note of them and bring your attention back to experiencing the moment with your body and paying attention to the physical sensations of temperature, pressure, and texture.

It is recommended that you lie side by side and relax for a few moments after you have completed the exercise, but not to talk about it immediately afterwards so that the discussion around evaluating does not affect your ability to stay with the sensations and experience. You are also not to discuss your feelings, thoughts, or experience with each other during the touching session.

After you have reflected on the exercise, both partners should take some time to <u>write down</u> what the experience was like. Reflect on things such as what it was like to make time for it and plan it, what it was like to be the toucher and the touchee, and which one you preferred. What kinds of touch did you prefer and what parts of your body did you like being touched on? Was it easy to follow the instructions? What thoughts or memories came up for you during? What were the main feelings that you were aware of? Did you feel bored, excited, connected, relaxed, self-conscious, anxious? And how did you feel about your partner and your own body after the exercise? What distractions came up and how did you manage them?

Incorporating the Partner   103

Take a few moments after your reflection to discuss with each other how the exercise felt as you were the toucher and the touchee – share your experience on what you enjoyed and what did not feel comfortable for you.

There are a couple of rules to keep while practicing Stage 1 of Sensate Focus in order to get the best out of the program:

<u>No talking during the exercise.</u> *Do not discuss relevant or irrelevant matters during the exercise, and do not influence each other by giving feedback or providing guidance. As mentioned previously, this exercise is just as much for the benefit of the person who is touching as it is for the one receiving the touch, and it gives the toucher an opportunity to freely and actively experience and explore their partner's body in a tactile and visual way. You might feel apprehensive about the exercise before starting the touching session. You may talk about your feelings with your partner before or after the exercise but not during. If you feel uncomfortable or giggly during the touching, bring your attention to the physical sensations and try to sit through the discomfort until it passes. However, if anything is too uncomfortable or unbearable for the touchee (ticklish, sensitive, or intensely emotionally triggering), you should tell your partner to switch or change, or take their hand and guide it to a different area. You can then experiment with other ways of touching that feel better.*

<u>No sex during or after the exercise.</u> *One or both of you may feel aroused during the exercise due to the touch and intimacy (though if you do not feel aroused do not worry, it does not always happen and that is not necessarily expected), but the exercise still ends once you both complete 15 minutes of touching and being touched. If you would like to relieve yourself, you may masturbate on your own afterwards, but you are not to engage in vaginal penetrative sex or other sexual activities together right after the exercise, even if you want to. The reason behind this is that, by banning sex and genital stimulation, we are removing the pressure to perform (and any performance anxiety associated with that), and any expectations or anxiety linked to the possibility of having sex, thus creating a safety to relax and focus on being mindful and present during the exercise. Another reason behind this is to promote other forms of intimacy so that you can learn to focus on the sensations and connection rather than always thinking of PIV sex or orgasm as the goal.*

A few words about the exercise:

It is very important that you are consistent with this exercise and practice it three times a week for at least two weeks. If you are unable to practice it three times a week, then I would suggest you practice it twice a week for three weeks. Do not move on to the next stage before at least two weeks of consistent practice, and more importantly, before you both feel relaxed and comfortable during the exercise, and have learned to focus on your sensations in a curious and exploratory manner.

104 *Incorporating the Partner*

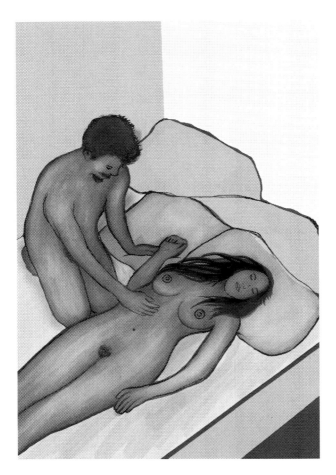

Figure 6.1 Sensate Focus Stage 1.

It is very common for it to feel awkward at first, and for it to even feel like a task/ obligation rather than something you are looking forward to. Do not let this put you off from doing it because this program tends to have a cumulative effect – the benefits show up a bit later, so you have to trust the process. Learning to be more comfortable with each other, in addition to being more present and immersed in the experience, while not being allowed to engage in sexual activity during, create a build-up of excitement and more enjoyment that you will experience at a later stage in this process.

Moving forward, whenever you proceed with the more advanced step, please remember to build up the exercise based on the previous step. For example, do not just jump straight into Stage 2, but rather start with a few moments or minutes of Stage 1 and then build up to the instructions of the next stage as you get more comfortable during the session.

Stage 2

Once you have completed at least two weeks practicing Stage 1 three times a week, and only if the exercise has become a comfortable experience for you both, you can proceed to Stage 2. Please do not proceed if you still do not feel relaxed or comfortable in Stage 1. Instead, go back to Stage 1 and practice it a few more times until you are both more relaxed and you have learned to manage distractions during by bringing your attention back to the physical sensations. Remember that you do not need to have enjoyed Stage 1 in order to proceed. At this point we are less interested in producing pleasurable or positive emotions and experiences, and more focused on just the ability to get comfortable with touch and being able to reduce the anxiety around sex by paying attention to the sensations of pressure, temperature, and texture.

Stage 2 is similar to Stage 1, with the addition of giving each other feedback during the exercise. Follow the same instructions as for Stage 1, but now you are allowed to speak to each other throughout the exercise, specifically regarding how it feels, or to take your partner's hand and guide it, or to make sounds that express your sensations. Make sure that you do not end up having long conversations, especially about things that are irrelevant, so that you can still be present and focused on the experience and sensations. You may give your partner feedback on how the touch feels and if you would like something different, but do not take complete control. Remember that it does not mean that your partner must follow your guidance – they are still free to choose how they would like to touch you (as long as they respect your limits). The feedback is to be focused on the physical sensations, and not on the thoughts or emotions you may have during, as we still want to practice learning to pay attention to the physical experience.

Make sure that your feedback is not coming over as commands (giving orders), but rather as requests or observations. For example, avoid sentences like "go harder" or "do more of this" and instead use sentences more like "I would prefer harder strokes" or "this feels smooth." As in Stage 1, reflect on the experience and process it once you are done, and practice it three times a week for at least one to two weeks or until it feels more relaxing and comfortable.

Once you have completed Stage 2 and you are both feeling more and more relaxed and comfortable with the exercise, you may move on to Stage 3. Remember that even though you might still feel like the process is mechanical or you are not very excited about it before starting it, stay committed to the program and work through feeling more comfortable with being touched and touching. Also, if you do feel aroused during (which is still not necessary), remember that you are not supposed to have sex or pleasure each other to orgasm during or after the exercise.

(If you are experiencing any negative or distressing emotions that are not getting resolved with more practice, I recommend that you consult a professional before continuing.)

Stage 3

Stage 3 again is similar to Stage 2, and you may now touch each other's sexual areas. Similarly, after completing Stage 2, begin Stage 3 by spending a few moments in the session building on Stage 2 rather than immediately starting with touching each other's sexual areas. Please note that you may not sexually pleasure each other yet, therefore, the rule of no sexual activity (PIV sex or sexual activities with the intent to produce orgasm) still applies, even though you might get aroused. You may only touch each other with the intent to explore and focus on the sensations of touching, but not with the intent of giving your partner an orgasm. Therefore, the toucher may not insert fingers into the touchee's vagina yet, and may not manually stimulate the female clitoris or the male penis in a masturbatory fashion. You do not need to withhold or suppress any excited or aroused feelings, as it is natural for your body to respond in that way to your sexual areas being touched. In fact, pleasurable sensations and feelings through sensual touch are encouraged – we just want to make sure that the intent behind the touch is exploratory, focused, and sensual rather than orgasm-producing.

If your arousal level becomes too distracting or you start to focus on the goal of achieving orgasm, then shift your attention back to the physical sensations of texture, pressure, and temperature. If you are finding that difficult and your arousal is overpowering the experience, then either verbally request that the toucher changes the location or style of touching, or take his hand and gently guide it to another less sexually arousing area. And if the visual input becomes too stimulating and distracting, you are encouraged to close your eyes.

It is also possible for some people to become orgasmic during this exercise. If that happens, do not worry. Just as becoming aroused can be a natural response to being touched or touching sexual areas, so can experiencing an orgasm happen. As long as achieving orgasm was not the intention of the person and it happened as a natural response, you may continue with the Sensate Focus session and bring your attention back to the sensations. If any ejaculation happened, you may dry it off with a towel and continue with the session. An orgasmic response during the exercise is especially the time to NOT stop the session in order to reinforce the idea that nothing specific needs to happen as a result of orgasm, pleasure, or any other specific sexual response.

As with Stages 1 and 2, gently tell your partner if anything feels uncomfortable, and of course you may also give each other feedback on the sensations you are experiencing. Take a few moments to reflect on the experience afterwards and write things down. Practice this stage three times a week for at least two weeks as well, or until it feels comfortable. It may feel awkward or exposing at first, which may indicate that you and your partner have still not developed enough closeness and safety yet, but continuing to practice it and taking things gradually usually helps in overcoming the discomfort and enjoying it more.

<u>Stage 4</u>

As with all previous stages, make sure you are feeling comfortable and relaxed enough in the previous stage before moving onto this one, and start with the previous Sensate Focus sequences first. Stage 4 is similar to Stage 3 with the addition of being allowed to manually pleasure each other (without having PIV sex yet) by touching each other's genitals to arouse. With no pressure to perform or achieve orgasm, let yourselves go, and enjoy the touch and sensations. It is not a must to achieve orgasm, so it is important to remember to keep the focus on the sensuality and be present in the moment rather than focusing on achieving orgasm. You are also free to guide your partner with your hand and give them feedback (gently and without giving orders or instructions). You may also touch each other simultaneously instead of taking turns, but remember that mutual touching does not have to happen all the time.

Practice this stage three times a week for at least two weeks as well, or for longer until you feel relaxed and are enjoying it and being able to be present. If you still feel uncomfortable or are not enjoying it yet, I suggest you go back to Stage 3 and practice that a few more times before progressing to this stage again.

This is not the end of the Sensate Focus program; however, this stage will be the last one for the client to complete at this point in the treatment process. I usually prefer to work through the genital exposure steps with the partner before moving on to the genital-to-genital contact stages of Sensate Focus.

Partner-Assisted Genital Exposure

Hopefully by now the client should be feeling much more comfortable with her genital area, and find the idea and sensation of penetration to be more agreeable. In addition, having gone through the emotional exercises and some of the Sensate Focus sessions, the client is hopefully feeling more connected and sexually aroused with her partner. Once again, I find that celebrating all the steps and milestones of progress, no matter how small, is valuable for the client to remain hopeful and motivated. It is now time for the client to move on to the next level and start progressing with experiences that will prepare her for penetration specifically with and by her partner. The series of these steps are similar to the solo genital exposure progressions the client practiced on her own (inserting her fingers), except that now the partner will be progressively inserting his fingers.

108   *Incorporating the Partner*

Couples Genital Exposure Worksheet

Similar to your solo genital exposure progressions program, the first step of the genital desensitization program with your partner is to practice gradually getting more comfortable with feeling your partner's finger(s) around and on your vulva, and inside your vagina. Begin by working up to Stage 3 of the Sensate Focus program (page 106) again in order for you to get into the mood, feel relaxed, and build up some arousal. Before your partner makes any attempts, it can be a good idea for you to "warm up" your genital area by touching your vulva for a few moments as you focus on your sensations like in Step 5 of the Self-Sensate program (page 86), and build up to inserting your own finger(s).

Using a similar approach to what you have done so far, when you feel your body is ready, start by having him place his hand on the outside of your genital area and keep his hand still there for a few moments or a couple of minutes until you relax. While his hand is on your vulva, practice some of the breathing and relaxation techniques we have covered so that you fully relax. Only when your discomfort or anxiety has dissipated can he remove his hand and you may end this session. Practice this step a few times over a week or more (depending on how much you need) until you are ready for him to attempt inserting the tip of his forefinger.

Once you feel comfortable with your partner's hand touching your vulva, you may start focusing on building up to him inserting the tip of his finger. If his forefinger feels too stressful or difficult at this point in time, you may begin with his pinky instead, and once you have achieved full penetration of his pinky, then go through these same steps again using his forefinger. While you are sitting up or lying down in bed, and after having built up some arousal through Stage 3 of Sensate Focus, have your partner place the tip of his forefinger on your vaginal opening (as shown in Figure 6.2), just like you did in the early stages of your solo genital exposure progressions (page 89). Remember to breathe into it until you relax. If it helps you feel safer or more in control, feel free to hold his hand as he places the tip of his finger on your vaginal opening.

If you are ready, you may guide his hand with your hand on how to insert the tip since you have already done so yourself, and have him insert just the tip. Once he has inserted the tip, keep it in for a few moments, practice some of the breathing and relaxation exercises, and when you have settled and feel more comfortable, he may remove it. If you are not ready to insert the tip yet, just keep his finger on your vaginal opening without penetrating, and breathe deeply into it until you relax. You may end the session once your discomfort and anxiety has dissipated, and practice that several times over the next week or two until you are ready to attempt inserting the tip of his finger. Keep in mind the importance of being sufficiently sexually aroused, not only in terms of a healthy sexual response, but also in order to have a smoother insertion. Therefore, if you feel your arousal level is

Incorporating the Partner 109

Figure 6.2 Man touching his female partner's vulva.

not enough and your genitals are not sufficiently lubricated and relaxed, then it is a good idea to go back to previous Sensate Focus stages to build up the touch, sensations, and arousal.

Keep practicing this twice or three times a week, and attempt to go a little bit further each time (guiding his finger with your hand) until you are able to insert his whole finger. Only attempt to progress with the depth of penetration if the stage you currently are practicing feels comfortable and your anxiety has dissipated. Follow a similar approach to the one that worked for you during your solo genital exposure progressions, which means that you will probably be able to insert a quarter of his finger, followed by a third of his finger, then half of his finger, until you are able to insert his finger fully. Take as many days and weeks as you need as you attempt this every two to three days. This is not a process you should rush, and remember to go back a step or two if you feel stuck or very stressed. Communicate with your partner about how you are feeling and if you would like him to do something differently. Also remember that you can use the Kegel exercises as a way to consciously relax your pelvic muscles in order to allow for a smoother and easier penetration.

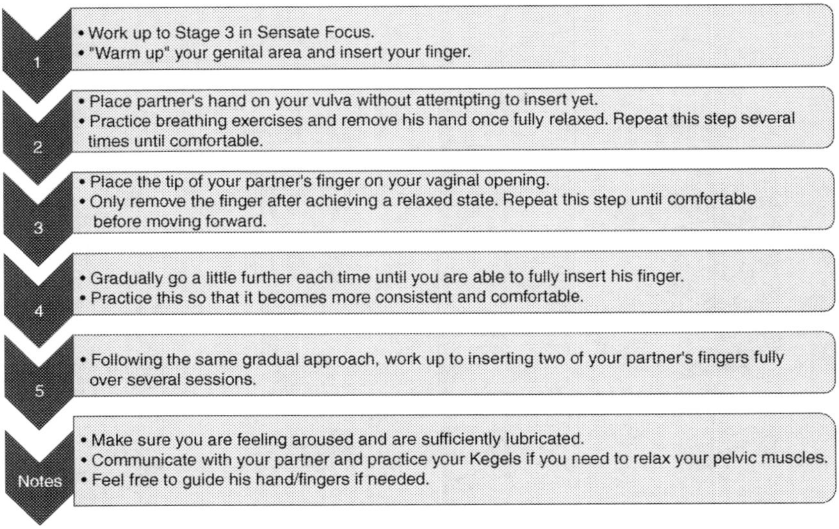

110 *Incorporating the Partner*

1
- Work up to Stage 3 in Sensate Focus.
- "Warm up" your genital area and insert your finger.

2
- Place partner's hand on your vulva without attemtpting to insert yet.
- Practice breathing exercises and remove his hand once fully relaxed. Repeat this step several times until comfortable.

3
- Place the tip of your partner's finger on your vaginal opening.
- Only remove the finger after achieving a relaxed state. Repeat this step until comfortable before moving forward.

4
- Gradually go a little further each time until you are able to fully insert his finger.
- Practice this so that it becomes more consistent and comfortable.

5
- Following the same gradual approach, work up to inserting two of your partner's fingers fully over several sessions.

Notes
- Make sure you are feeling aroused and are sufficiently lubricated.
- Communicate with your partner and practice your Kegels if you need to relax your pelvic muscles.
- Feel free to guide his hand/fingers if needed.

Figure 6.3 Partner-assisted genital exposure flowchart.

> When one finger feels easy enough to move forward, you may attempt to insert his forefinger and middle finger together (starting with the tips and guiding his fingers with your hand). As always, follow a progressive approach where you practice these sessions every two to three days and attempt to go a little further once your anxiety subsides. Similarly to the solo genital exposure progressions, the goal is to insert two of your partner's fingers comfortably, before attempting PIV sex. With practice, patience, and communication, you will be able to insert his fingers. Figure 6.3 summarizes these progressions.
>
> For some of the women I worked with, inserting one finger was sufficient to build their confidence and train their vagina to a level where they can move forward to the next stages, whereas for others, they needed to insert two of his fingers. Since each woman and each case is different, I encourage you to tune in to yourself and honor what you feel you need. Remember that you can always go back to previous steps if you decide to move forward and experience significant challenges. If at any point throughout the partner-assisted genital exposure progressions you feel stuck or are experiencing increasing levels of difficulty, then I highly recommend you consult a qualified sex therapist.

Case Example

> Iman, who had to learn to be more patient and trust the process, eventually encountered some challenges with the partner exercises as well. Adding a partner into the mix creates another level of difficulty for the client, which is learning to

trust someone else. This can be especially challenging for clients who find it hard to let go of being in total control. Once again, I needed to slow things down and work on some of the harsh and unrealistic expectations she had of herself and her partner, and to continuously encourage and support her through listening to and trusting her body. At times, this meant that they needed to take a step back and practice the previous exercise again for a week or two until they built more trust and confidence, and she felt relaxed enough to let go. I find that it is just as important to work with the partner on learning to trust his intuition in those moments as well, as he often would feed off of her anxiety and feel her resistance. Their behaviors would often mirror each other's feelings, and so it may be helpful to acknowledge their feelings and difficulties as they come up, communicate with each other what they need, and modify the practice/exercise accordingly.

Reaching this far in the treatment process is huge, and for some women more than enough to be able to achieve penetration and have vaginal penetrative sex. Depending on her history, the intensity of her discomfort to begin with, and the quality of her relationship with her partner, she may be feeling confident enough and sufficiently aroused to be able to have vaginal intercourse with her partner comfortably. As a professional, I feel it is important for us to guide her in assessing where she is at in terms of her relationship with her genitals and her partner, and how ready she truly is, as opposed to how ready she "thinks" she is or wants to be. Sometimes clients prematurely jump to the next step because they are feeling impatient, anxious, and/or receiving pressure from their families. Even if she does attempt to jump forward, we can always reassure her that she can take it a step back again if she did so prematurely. Once she and her partner have been able to navigate inserting her and his fingers more easily, and before they attempt PIV sex, I suggest they go through the last stages of Sensate Focus as a way to transition more safely and comfortably to penetrative sex.

Completing the Process

Sensate Focus: Stage 5

After you have both achieved a place where you are enjoying the experience, feeling relaxed and comfortable with touching each other and being touched, you may now move on to Stage 5 of the Sensate Focus program which includes genital-to-genital contact without insertion. As always, it is highly recommended that you include all previous positions in the sequence of the program to build up the mindful touch and experience without the pressure to perform. Once you have built up to Stage 4, you may take on the position of being on top, hovering over your partner with your knees on the bed and supporting yourself with your knees close to your partner's body (as shown in Figure 6.4). You will also be using your non-dominant hand to support yourself in a tripod position as if you are on a horse but without directly sitting on your partner.

112 *Incorporating the Partner*

Figure 6.4 Woman hovering on top of her male partner.

Use your other hand and your partner's genitals which are directly below yours to explore vulvar and clitoral contact and sensations but without insertion. Remember to maintain the intention of touching while focusing on your own sensations and self-interest. Your partner, who is on the bottom, must refrain from moving his hips and let the partner on top lead the genital-to-genital contact while also focusing on the sensations. When you (on top) start to feel tired and are not able to maintain your hovering position much longer, you may switch positions and go back to earlier stages that include mutual touching or taking turns touching. Go back to the hovering position with genital-to-genital contact without insertion once or twice more.

<u>Sensate Focus: Stage 6</u>

When you feel ready to take it to the last step, Stage 6 allows you to transition to attempting vaginal penetrative sex. However, please keep in mind that it is very important for you to approach it in a similar manner as previous Sensate Focus steps, where the priority is to pay attention to the sensations and sensuality, and be present in the moment, without the pressure to perform or achieve orgasm. Be careful not to fall back into the mindset of having PIV sex as the primary goal, as this can lead to feeling pressured and stressed about the experience. It is also completely OK for you to refuse vaginal penetrative sex if you are not up for it, and just go back to Stage 4 or 5 until you are.

Before attempting penetration, I strongly suggest that you build up the experience and sexual arousal first by practicing Stage 4, and then inserting his finger (followed by his two fingers) into your vagina, to warm up your genital area and desensitize it. Once you feel ready, move on to Stage 5, and then you may attempt PIV sex. Remember that when it comes to vaginismus, as previously discussed, it is very important for you (the woman) to be in control of the process.

Therefore, in Stage 6 when attempting vaginal penetrative sex, I strongly recommend that you begin with positions, such as in Stage 5, where you are in control of the movements and the method and depth of penetration. For example, many women prefer the female superior position where they are on top, as they are able to control the depth and the movements, rather than the man being on top and in control. If you do not like being on top and feel more comfortable in a missionary position (him on top with you lying on your back), that is fine, but I still recommend that you find other positions that make you feel more in control, or take charge of part of it by guiding his penis inside your vagina with your hand.

Before you attempt to penetrate, firstly just place the tip of the penis on your vaginal opening (similar to the first step before inserting your finger), without attempting to insert it. You must make it very clear to your partner that he is not supposed to insert it until you initiate it and give him permission to do so. Hold this position for a few moments, breathe into it, and you may end the session once you have relaxed into it. If you get tired holding this position you may take a break and resume the position until you feel relaxed and your discomfort has dissipated.

After you have become more comfortable with this position and penis-vaginal opening contact over a few sessions of practice (throughout a week or two), you may attempt to insert the tip of his penis. Guide his penis with your hand to a comfortable angle. In addition, some women find it easier to be on top as they can control the movements better, but if you prefer to be in missionary position then make sure you are setting the pace and guiding your partner on what you are ready for. Remember to always follow the same protocol of keeping the tip inside for a few moments or minutes until your anxiety subsides before you end the session.

It is generally preferred if you are sufficiently aroused and lubricated while attempting these progressions of penis-into-vagina insertion. If you find that you are not wet enough, thus making the penetration more difficult, I would *recommend that you shift the focus back to the sensual touch, build up more arousal, excitement, and pleasure, before you continue. And if you are still finding it difficult to experience or achieve sufficient lubrication or arousal at this stage despite the sensual and sexual touch you are engaging in with your partner, then I suggest you consult a qualified sex therapist, especially if the lack of lubrication is leading to pain.*

Once you have been able to consistently insert the tip of the penis into your vaginal entry, try to go a little bit deeper in each session that you practice, until your partner is able to fully penetrate. Follow a gradual approach similar to the one we went through with inserting the fingers where you take it just a little further in each session rather than attempting full penetration immediately. Throughout the whole process please remember to, firstly, take the lead regarding how much your partner will penetrate, and secondly, maintain each position for a few moments as you practice deep breathing until the discomfort subsides before you end the session or move on to a deeper progression. Once you have been able to receive full penetration, maintain the position with his penis inside your vagina for a few moments as you breathe deeply and relax into it. Do not start thrusting as if you are engaging in vaginal penetrative sex just yet. If he loses his erection or some of his fullness while you are holding this position, that is OK. Remember that you are still focusing on the sensations and the present moment, regardless of the outcome.

This is a huge milestone in your journey! Let us celebrate how far you have come, all the challenges, discomfort, and fears you have worked through, and all the confidence within yourself and connection with your partner you have built. From this point onwards, your partner may gently thrust after penetration if you feel ready for that (as shown in Figure 6.5), and make sure to keep the lines of communication between the two of you open.

If, at this stage, you still feel blocked or intensely uncomfortable that you are unable to gradually progress to full penetration, despite having gone back to previous stages and practiced consistently, then I highly recommend that you consult a professional to help you overcome whatever is preventing you from moving forward.

When the client has successfully practiced Stage 6 and achieved full penetration, then she has completed treatment. I believe it is also important to assess whether she is feeling more relaxed and comfortable with her sensuality and sexuality, and more connected to her partner. My definition of successful treatment does not just depend on her being able to consummate her marriage. Seeing that I approach sexuality from a more holistic and integrated way, I believe it is just as valuable in terms of success for her to feel more positive about her body, to have established a healthier relationship with sex, and to experience arousal and pleasure. Nonetheless, I do not

Incorporating the Partner 115

Figure 6.5 Couple making love.

impose my view of success onto my clients, and so if they are satisfied with the work they have done and the status of their relationship and their sexual experiences, then I would consider treatment to have been successful and complete.

Conclusion

Closing Words and Beyond

I hope that you learned some of the main mental, emotional, relational, and physical themes related to sexuality, specifically GPPPD, in order to help clients overcome their penetration difficulties. Throughout the book, I have explored the key elements of my integrated approach to treating penetration disorders in women, which begins with identifying, challenging, and modifying their negative and unrealistic beliefs about sex. Next, I support the client through building confidence, assertiveness, and living more authentically. Additionally, I explore and suggest ways for the client to have a trusting, safe, and deeply emotionally connected relationship with her partner. I also provide the client with exercises and opportunities to familiarize herself with her body, connect with it more positively, and progressively expose herself to increasing degrees of dilation. And lastly, we discuss safe approaches for the couple to create sexual intimacy and gradually build up to vaginal penetrative sex.

Though the focus of this book is not around pleasure and orgasm, I would highly encourage clients to also learn to connect more with their own pleasure, for example, through self-pleasuring practices. For those who are curious about taking this work further, I would invite them to explore ways to expand their sexual inventory, experiences, and openness. Some of the things that can help clients do that are reading erotic material to stimulate some new interests. One of the books I recommend for that is *My Secret Garden* by Nancy Friday. Women can read it on their own or with their partners if they would like to explore their fantasies, imagery, and create novelty within the sexual relationship. Another area, of course, would be to enrich women's and men's literacy around female pleasure and orgasm so that sex is not only about consummating the relationship or procreation, but also about pleasure, sensuality, playfulness, and a sense of aliveness. The book *Becoming Orgasmic*, by Julia Heiman, PhD, and Joseph LoPiccolo, PhD, which I referenced a few times, is a self-help book for women to learn to experience more pleasure and orgasm, that I think would be a great start for that journey. Other books, such as *The Mirror Within* by Anne Dickson, *Come As You Are* by Emily Nagoski, PhD, and *Becoming Cliterate* by Dr. Laurie Mintz, are great resources for women to deepen their knowledge and connection with their sexuality and pleasure, and for their partners to learn more about them.

Nowadays it has become easier to find information online around sexuality, eroticism, kink, and more, and so I would encourage people to follow sex therapists, sexologists, and other credible sexual health experts on social media. Some of the ones I follow are @estherperelofficial and @sexwithdrjess and @thesexdoctor on Instagram, for content. Be sure to check out their books as well (*The Ultimate Guide to Seduction and Foreplay* by Dr. Jessica O'Reilly and Marla Renee Stewart; *Mind the Gap* by Dr. Karen Gurney). Esther Perel is a world-renowned expert in the field of sex therapy with wonderful books to help couples understand the intricacies around desire (her book *Mating in Captivity* is a must-read). Speaking of desire, the work of Dr. Rosemary Basson is key in challenging and reframing the traditional views of female dysfunction and sexual desire, which I believe all women and men need to be educated on.

Couples can also go beyond what this book offers and learn more about how to strengthen their relationship and nurture their connection further. In addition to Harville Hendrix, PhD, and Helen LaKelly Hunt, PhD, previously mentioned, the works of Drs. John and Julie Gottman and Dr. Sue Johnson are great resources. Couples can learn more about what contributes to a happy marriage and how to be more emotionally available to each other. The book *Passionate Marriage* by David Schnarch, PhD (who sadly passed away as I was completing the manuscript) is an amazing resource, especially regarding how to create passion by being differentiated and connected in a relationship. I am also a huge fan of couples' workshops, intensives, and retreats. I offer some myself, but there are also many Imago couples' workshops and Gottman workshops around the world. Additionally, there are many online courses for individuals and couples on various topics in the sexuality and relationship realms.

I hope that putting together my clinical experience will help clinicians, therapists, gynecologists, and other health practitioners gain a deeper understanding of the topic, develop more empathy, become more culturally informed, and learn new skills and tools to provide their clients with the care they need. And I hope that this book serves as a useful resource for women to create a more compassionate and confident relationship with themselves and their sexual bodies, whether they read this on their own or work with a professional in overcoming their difficulties. If a woman followed this as a self-help book and is still experiencing difficulty, or would like to enhance her relationship even further, seeking help from a professional is not only advisable, but also admirable. I feel a great deal of fulfillment as I work with clients through their journey of overcoming some very difficult experiences and doing a lot of inner work, and share their joy when they experience the sexual and emotional relationship they want with themselves and their partners. I would choose this career all over again.

Conclusion: Closing Words and Beyond

I often think about how different the world would be if we were not made to feel ashamed of our bodies and desires, and how that would affect the way we connect to ourselves and others. Unfortunately, we cannot change the past and undo the things we have been told or exposed to, but we do have some power over how we relate to our bodies, our sexuality, and other people today. We have an impact on others by being who we are and expressing ourselves the way we do. And so I feel we have a responsibility to heal ourselves and grow, so that we can create a safer world for others to exist and express themselves as well. We also have an effect on and a responsibility toward our children and other people's children, whether it is through social interactions or our jobs. Thus, we have a huge opportunity to model for future generations what we want to see in this world.

Part of the change is therefore not only to eliminate the shame around sex and provide sex-neutral education, but to also learn and share sex-positive material and education. This includes normalizing different forms of sexual expression, recognizing the importance and beauty of giving and receiving pleasure, and empowering us to choose what to say yes or no to. This might be difficult to hear for some people, but for the sake of continuing to push boundaries, as I clearly love to do, I hope to one day see a world where men and women, especially women from my part of the world, own their sexuality and feel safe to explore it freely (I feel proud and hopeful as I see some progress in the availability of sexual health information in Arabic, such as the previously mentioned Instagram account @mauj.me). I guess by doing this work and helping shift people's relationship with sex, one client at a time, I am attempting to do my part in creating this world. I hope you will join me in this vision!

References

Akhtar, N., Khan, A., Pervez, A., & Batool, I. (2017). Interpersonal Problems in Arranged and Love Marriages. Pakistan Journal of Social and Clinical Psychology. 15. 18–22.

American Psychiatric Association. (2000). Diagnostic and statistical manual of mental disorders (4th ed.). Washington, DC: American Psychiatric Association.

American Psychiatric Association. (2013). Diagnostic and statistical manual of mental disorders (5th ed.). Washington, DC: American Psychiatric Association.

Badran, W., Moamen, N., Fahmy, I., El-Karaksy, A., Abdel-Nasser, T., & Ghanem, H. (2006). Etiological Factors of Unconsummated Marriage. International Journal of Impotence Research. 18. 458–63. 10.1038/sj.ijir.3901452.

Bancroft, J., Loftus, J., & Long, J.S. (2003). Distress About Sex: A National Survey of Women in Heterosexual Relationships. Archives of Sexual Behavior. 32. 193–208. 10.1023/A:1023420431760.

Basson, R., Leiblum, S., Brotto, L., Derogatis, L., Fourcroy, J., Fugl-Meyer, K., Graziottin, A., Heiman, J., Laan, E., Meston, C., Schover, L., van Lankveld, J., & Schultz, W.W. (2004). Revised Definitions of Women's Sexual Dysfunction. Journal of Sexual Medicine. 1. 40–8. 10.1111/j.1743-6109.2004.10107.x.

Batabyal, A., & Beladi, H. (2002). Arranged or Love Marriage? That Is the Question. Applied Economics Letters. 9. 893–7. 10.2139/ssrn.312152.

Bokaie, M., Bostani Khalesi, Z., & Yasini-Ardekani, S. (2017). Diagnosis and Treatment of Unconsummated Marriage in an Iranian Couple. African Health Sciences. 17. 632. 10.4314/ahs.v17i3.5.

Borg, C., & Jong, P. (2012). Feelings of Disgust and Disgust-Induced Avoidance Weaken following Induced Sexual Arousal in Women. PloS one. 7. e44111. 10.1371/journal.pone.0044111.

Borg, C., Peters, M., & Schultz, W.W., & Jong, P. (2012). Vaginismus: Heightened Harm Avoidance and Pain Catastrophizing Cognitions. Journal of Sexual Medicine. 9. 558–67. 10.1111/j.1743-6109.2011.02535.x.

Brauer, M., Lakeman, M., van Lunsen, R., & Laan, E. (2014). Predictors of Task-Persistent and Fear-Avoiding Behaviors in Women with Sexual Pain Disorders. Journal of Sexual Medicine. 11. 10.1111/jsm.12697.

Chapman, G.D. (1995). The five love languages: How to express heartfelt commitment to your mate. Chicago: Northfield Pub.

Christianson, M., & Eriksson, C. (2013). Myths and Misconceptions: Midwives' Perception of the Vaginal Opening or Hymen and Virginity. British Journal of Midwifery. 21. 108–15. 10.12968/bjom.2013.21.2.108.

Cinthio, H. (2015). "You go home and tell that to my dad!" Conflicting Claims and Understandings on Hymen and Virginity. Sexuality & Culture. 19. 10.1007/s12119-014-9253-2.

Fadul, R., Garcia, R., Zapata-Boluda, R., Aranda-Pastor, C., Brotto, L., Parron-Carreño, T., & Alarcon-Rodriguez, R. (2019). Psychosocial Correlates of Vaginismus Diagnosis: A Case-Control Study. Journal of Sex & Marital Therapy. 45:1. 73–83. 10.1080/0092623X.2018.1484401.

Farnam, F., Janghorbani, M., Khoei, E., & Raisi, F. (2014). Vaginismus and Its Correlates in an Iranian Clinical Sample. International Journal of Impotence Research. 26. 10.1038/ijir.2014.16.

Gurney, K. (2020). Mind the Gap: The truth about desire and how to futureproof your sex life. London: Headline.

Heiman, J., & LoPiccolo, J. (1988). Becoming orgasmic: A sexual and personal growth program for women. New York: Prentice Hall.

Hendrix, H. (1990). Getting the love you want: A guide for couples. New York: Perennial Library.

Hendrix, H. (2005). Keeping the love you find: A single person's guide to achieving lasting love. London: Pocket.

Klein, V., Koops, T., Lange, C., & Briken, P. (2015). Sexual History of Male Partners of Women with the Diagnosis Vaginismus. Sexual and Relationship Therapy. 30. 1–9. 10.1080/14681994.2015.1025183.

KSLatha, Madhyastha, S., Bhat, S.M., & Haridas, K. (2013). Unconsummated Marriage and its Etiological Factors: A Case Series. Middle East Journal of Psychiatry and Alzheimers. 4. 10.5742/MEJPA.2013.42290.

La Rocque, C., & Cioe, J. (2011). An Evaluation of the Relationship between Body Image and Sexual Avoidance. Journal of Sex Research. 48. 397–408. 10.1080/00224499.2010.499522.

Lahaie, M-A., Boyer, S., Amsel, R., Khalifé, S., & Binik, Y. (2010). Vaginismus: A Review of the Literature on the Classification/Diagnosis, Etiology and Treatment. Women's Health. 6. 705–19. 10.2217/whe.10.46.

Lau, J., Kim, J., & Tsui, H-Y. (2005). Prevalence of Male and Female Sexual Problems, Perceptions Related to Sex and Association with Quality of Life in a Chinese Population: A Population-Based Study. International Journal of Impotence Research. 17. 494–505. 10.1038/sj.ijir.3901342.

Laumann, E., Paik, A., & Rosen, R.C. (1999). Sexual dysfunction in the United States: Prevalence and predictors. JAMA: The Journal of the American Medical Association. 281. 537–44.

Leiblum, S. (ed.). (2007). Principles and practice of sex therapy (4th ed.). New York: Guildford Press.

McNicoll, G., Corsini-Munt, S., Rosen, N., Mcduff, P., & Bergeron, S. (2016). Sexual Assertiveness Mediates the Associations Between Partner Facilitative Responses and Sexual Outcomes in Women With Provoked Vestibulodynia. Journal of Sex and Marital Therapy. 43. 10.1080/0092623X.2016.1230806.

Michetti, P., Silvaggi, M., Fabrizi, A., Tartaglia, N., Rossi, R., & Simonelli, C. (2013). Unconsummated Marriage: Can It Still Be Considered a Consequence of Vaginismus? International Journal of Impotence Research. 26. 10.1038/ijir.2013.24.

References

Muammar, T., Mcwalter, P., Alkhenizan, A., Shoukri, M., Gabr, A., & Bin, A. (2015). Management of Vaginal Penetration Phobia in Arab Women: A Retrospective Study. Annals of Saudi Medicine. 35. 120–6. 10.5144/0256-4947.2015.120.

Nagoski, E. (2015). Come as you are: The surprising new science that will transform your sex life. New York: Simon & Schuster.

Nobre, P., Pinto-Gouveia, J., & Gomes, F. (2006). Prevalence and Comorbidity of Sexual Dysfunctions in a Portuguese Clinical Sample. Journal of Sex & Marital Therapy. 32. 173–82. 10.1080/00926230500442334.

Oksuz, E., & Malhan, S. (2006). Prevalence and Risk Factors for Female Sexual Dysfunction in Turkish Women. Journal of Urology. 175. 654–8; discussion 658. 10.1016/S0022-5347(05)00149-7.

Perez S., & Binik Y.M. (2016). Vaginismus: "Gone", But Not Forgotten. Psychiatric Times. 33. 7. www.psychiatrictimes.com/view/vaginismus-gone-not-forgotten

Perez S., Brown C., Binik Y.M. (2016). Vaginismus: When Genito-Pelvic Pain/Penetration Disorder Makes Intercourse Seem Impossible. In: Lipshultz L., Pastuszak A., Goldstein A., Giraldi A., Perelman M. (eds.). Management of sexual dysfunction in men and women. New York: Springer. https://doi.org/10.1007/978-1-4939-3100-2_24

Reissing, E., Binik, Y., Khalifé, S., Cohen, D., & Amsel, R. (2004). Vaginal Spasm, Pain, and Behavior: An Empirical Investigation of the Diagnosis of Vaginismus. Archives of Sexual Behavior. 33. 5–17. 10.1023/B:ASEB.0000007458.32852.c8.

Reissing, E.D., Binik, Y.M., Khalif, S., Cohen, D., & Amsel, R. (2003). Etiological Correlates of Vaginismus: Sexual and Physical Abuse, Sexual Knowledge, Sexual Self-Schema, and Relationship Adjustment. Journal of Sex & Marital Therapy. 29:1. 47–59. 10.1080/713847095.

Rosen, N., Bergeron, S., Glowacka, M., Delisle, I., & Baxter, M. (2012). Harmful or Helpful: Perceived Solicitous and Facilitative Partner Responses Are Differentially Associated with Pain and Sexual Satisfaction in Women with Provoked Vestibulodynia. Journal of Sexual Medicine. 9. 2351–60. 10.1111/j.1743-6109.2012.02851.x.

Rubio, G. (2014). How love conquered marriage: Theory and evidence on the disappearance of arranged marriages. Unpublished manuscript. University of California, Merced.

Schnarch, D.M. (2009). Passionate marriage: Love, sex and intimacy in emotionally committed relationships. New York: W.W. Norton.

Tetik, S., Unlubilgin, E., Kayikcioglu, F., Meric, N., Boran, N., & Moraloglu, O. (2020). The Role of Anxiety and Childhood Trauma on Vaginismus and Its Comorbidity with Other Female Sexual Dysfunctions. International Journal of Sexual Health. 1–11. 10.1080/19317611.2020.1791297.

van Lankveld, J., & Grotjohann, Y. (2000). Psychiatric Comorbidity in Heterosexual Couples with Sexual Dysfunction Assessed with the Composite International Diagnostic Interview. Archives of Sexual Behavior. 29. 479–98. 10.1023/A:1001995704034.

Ward, E., & Ogden, J. (1994) Experiencing Vaginismus – Sufferers' Beliefs about Causes and Effects. Sexual and Relationship Therapy. 9:1. 33–45.

Weeks, G.R., Gambescia, N., & Hertlein, K.M. (2016). A clinician's guide to systemic sex therapy. Abingdon: Routledge.

Weiner, L., & Avery-Clark, C. (2017). Sensate focus in sex therapy: The illustrated manual. Abingdon: Routledge.

Yildirim, E., Hacioglu, M., & Karaş, H. (2019). Prevalence of Depression and Anxiety Disorders and Their Relationship with Sexual Functions in Women Diagnosed with Lifelong Vaginismus. Turkish Journal of Psychiatry. 30. 10.5080/u22858.

Zgueb, Y., Ouali, U., Achour, R., Jomli, R., & Nacef, F. (2019). Cultural Aspects of Vaginismus Therapy: A Case Series of Arab-Muslim Patients. The Cognitive Behaviour Therapist. 12. 10.1017/S1754470X18000119.

Index

Note: Page numbers in *italics* indicate figures.

abusive parenting style 5
acquired penetration disorders 7–8, 16–17
Active Listening Worksheet 64–67
age factors, presentation of penetration disorders 9
anus, genital exploration exercise 86
anxiety: vs. authenticity 48, 49, 51; cognitive behavioural therapy 21; and control 41; development of penetration disorders 6, 7; empowerment process 43; mindfulness 71; myths and unhealthy beliefs about sex 31; in partner 56; partner-assisted genital exposure 108, 109, 110, 111; perfectionists 51; presentation of penetration disorders 9, 17; progressive desensitization 74–75; relational factors 55; Sensate Focus 97, 99, 103, 105, 113
appreciated, feeling 63
Apps 71
Arab cultures 11–14, 21, 118
arousal: circuit 23–24, *24*; and desire, difference between 23; vs. disgust 37–38; partner-assisted genital exposure 108–109, 111; Sensate Focus 103, 105, 106, 107, 113–114
arranged marriages 38, 55; presentation of penetration disorders 11–13, 14
assertiveness 43–48, 51–52; assessment guidelines 44–45; and authenticity 50; communication skills 64; of partner 58–59; relational factors 57; training worksheet 45–48
attitude to sex 34, 35; worksheet 34–35

authenticity 48–50, 51–52, 53; and assertiveness 50; letting go 51; of partner 58, 59
authoritarian parenting style 5
Avery-Clark, C. 97, 100
avoidance, breaking the cycle of 98

Basson, Rosemary 2–3, 19, 117
bath: body image exercise 76–77; mindfulness exercise 79–80
Becoming Cliterate (Mintz) 116
Becoming Orgasmic (Heiman and LoPiccolo) 74, 116
bleeding and first sexual experience 26–27
body 69; mindfulness, relaxation, and grounding 71–74; pelvic floor strengthening 69–71; Self-Sensate program 74–89; solo genital exposure progressions 89–95
body awareness: through touch 80–82, *80*; through touch and sight 82–83
body exploration exercises 79–89
body image 69; Self-Sensate program 76–79, 77, 94
box breathing 73, *73*

Calm App 71
Chapman, Gary 63
"check ins" 68
children: desire to have 10; pressure to have 13; sexual abuse 5, 22, 39–40
Clinician's Guide to Systemic Sex Therapy, A (Weeks, Gambescia, and Hertlein) 97
clitoral hood: genital awareness through touch exercise 87; genital exploration exercise 85–86

Index

clitoris: genital awareness through touch exercise 87; genital exploration exercise 85–86; orgasms 30
cognitive behavioural therapy 21
Come As You Are (Nagoski) 27, 116
communication: about pain 57; partner-assisted genital exposure 109; problems, and development of penetration disorders 6; Sensate Focus 98, 114; skills 64–68
compassion 49
compulsive sexual behaviors 28
confidence: assertiveness 45, 48, 50, 52; authenticity 50, 52; of partner 56, 59; Self-Sensate program 75; therapeutic interventions 18
consent 33; sexual abuse 39–40
conservative and traditional cultures: development of penetration disorders 5; disgust 38; expectations around sex 22; inexperienced partners 55, 56; myths and unhealthy beliefs 26; presentation of penetration disorders 11–12, 14; sexual abuse 39
control 41; and anxiety 9; assertiveness 43–48; authenticity 48–50; letting go 50–53, 58–59; purpose of penetration disorders 41–43; Sensate Focus 113; sex as a condition for receiving love 32; sex as "doing to" someone 33
couples genital exposure worksheet 108–110
couples therapy 4, 19–20, 47, 55, 60–64
cultural taboos, and development of penetration disorders 5

defense mechanism, penetration disorders as a 42
depression, and presentation of penetration disorders 9
desensitization *see* progressive desensitization
desire: and arousal, difference between 23; fostered through Sensate Focus 99; spontaneous vs. responsive 27
development of penetration disorders 4–8
diagnosing penetration disorders 1, 2
Diagnostic and Statistical Manual of Mental Disorders: DSM-IV 1; DSM-V 2, 10
Dickson, Anne 43, 116
dilators 89

disgust 33, 36–38, 42; and sexual abuse 40; solo genital exposure progressions 90
divorce 13
"doing to" someone, sex as 32–33
dyspareunia: nature of 1, 3, 4; partner 56–57; presentation 9, 10; and vaginismus, difference between 4; *see also* pain

embarrassment, and unconsummated marriages 13
emotional abuse 58
empathy: authenticity 49; communication skills 66–67
empowerment 40, 43, 118; assertiveness 43–48, 57; authenticity 48–50; letting go 52; masturbation 28; relationship factors 59
erectile dysfunction 56; expectations around sex 23; unconsummated marriages 16
erotic material 116
exercises: body exploration 79–89; body image 76–79; box breathing 73, 73; five, four, three, two one 73–74; grounding 73–74; partner-assisted genital exposure 107–110; progressive muscular relaxation 72–73; relaxation 72–73; Self-Sensate 74–89; Sensate Focus 100–107, 111–114; solo genital exposure progressions 89–95
expectations around sex 22–24

familial taboos, and development of penetration disorders 5
fear: cognitive behavioural therapy 21; of losing control 5; myths and unhealthy beliefs about sex 25, 32; of pain 1–2, 3, 4, 7, 10, 23, 29, 57, 94; of penetration 69, 74; of pregnancy 6; presentation of penetration disorders 9; purpose of penetration disorders 42; relational factors 55; Self-Sensate program 75; and sexual abuse 40; of tearing 4; of the unknown 5, 94
finger insertion: by partner 107–111; solo 91–95
finger-on-vulva contact 89–90, 91
first sexual experience: bleeding 26–27; development of penetration disorders 5; expectations 22; myths and unhealthy beliefs 25, 26–27
five, four, three, two one exercise 73–74
Five Love Languages, The (Chapman) 63

foreplay 99
Friday, Nancy 116

Gambescia, N. 97
generalized penetration disorders 8
genital awareness through touch exercise 86–88, 87
genital exploration exercise 83–86
genital exposure, partner-assisted 107–111, 109; flowchart 110; worksheet 108–110
Getting the Love You Want (Hendrix) 64
Gibran, Gibran Khalil 59
Gottman, John, Julie and workshops 117
gradual exposure therapy 74
grounding 72; communication skills 65; exercise 73–74
guidelines: assertiveness assessment 44–45; Kegel exercises 70; mindfulness in daily life 71–72
guilt: vs. authenticity 48, 49; development of penetration disorders 5, 6; myths and unhealthy beliefs about sex 31; sexual abuse 40
Gurney, Karen 30, 117
gynecological examinations: conservative cultures 26; development of penetration disorders 6; generalized penetration disorders 8; presentation of penetration disorders 10, 16
gynecologists 2; dyspareunia 4; presentation of penetration disorders 15

Headspace App 71
Healthy Communication Worksheet 67–68
Heiman, Julia R. 74, 116
Hendrix, Harville 64, 117
Hertlein, K.M. 97
Hunt, Helen LaKelly 64, 117
hymen 25–26, 27; surgery 15, 26

Imago therapy 60, 64, 117
indirect messages about sex 34; worksheet 34–35
inexperienced partner 55–56; development of penetration disorders 6; presentation of penetration disorders 9, 14
Insight Timer App 71
Instagram 117
intensives 117

interest in sex 31–32
Islam: development of penetration disorders 5; sexual needs, fulfillment of 32

Johnson, Sue 117
Johnson, Virginia 97
journals 18; body awareness through touch and sight exercise 82–83; body image exercise 78; genital exploration exercise 86; Sensate Focus 102, 106

Keeping the Love You Find (Hendrix) 64
Kegel, Arnold 69
Kegel exercises 69–71; genital exploration exercise 86; partner-assisted genital exposure 109; solo genital exposure progressions 92
Keshet-Orr, Judi 61

labia: genital awareness through touch exercise 87; genital exploration exercise 83–84
letting go 50–53; relationship factors 58–59
lifelong penetration disorders 7–8; partner 56–57; presentation 16, 17
listening, active 64–67
LoPiccolo, Joseph 74, 116
love, sex as a condition for receiving 32
loved, feeling 63–64
love languages 63–64
love marriages 12, 13–14
lubricant 91, 92, 94

Martin, Betty, Wheel of Consent® 33
Master, William 97
masturbation 116; genital awareness through touch exercise 88; myths and unhealthy beliefs 28; Sensate Focus 103, 106
Mating in Captivity (Perel) 117
McNicoll, G. 57
medical examinations *see* gynecological examinations
meditation 71
menstruation 36, 37
Middle-Eastern cultures 11–14, 44
Miller, Jean 61
mindfulness 71–72, 95; bath exercise 79–80; body awareness through touch exercise 80–81; body image exercise 77; Sensate Focus 102, 103, 111; solo genital exposure progressions 89
Mind the Gap (Gurney) 30, 117

Mintz, Laurie 116
mirroring 65
Mirror Within, The (Dickson) 116
mons pubis/veneris, genital exploration exercise 83
Muslim women *see* Islam
My Secret Garden (Friday) 116
myths about sex 24–33

Nagoski, Emily 27, 116
nature of penetration disorders 2–4

online courses 117
O'Reilly, Jessica 117
orgasm 116; masturbation 28; myths and unhealthy beliefs 30–31; pelvic floor strengthening 70; Sensate Focus 106, 107, 113

pain: anticipatory 21; cycle 6, 7; development of penetration disorders 5–6, 7, 7; expectations around sex 22, 23; fear of 1–2, 3, 4, 7, 10, 23, 29, 57, 94; first sexual experience 22, 25; intimacy options 29–30; medical causes 5–6; myths and unhealthy beliefs 29–30, 31; presentation of penetration disorders 9, 10, 14; vulvar 57; *see also* dyspareunia
parenting style, and development of penetration disorders 5
partner: assessment of sexual history and function 55–56; effect of penetration disorders on 55; inexperienced *see* inexperienced partner; myths and unhealthy beliefs 29, 31, 32; presentation of penetration disorders 8, 9; role of 55–60; therapeutic interventions 17–18; *see also* relational factors; Sensate Focus
partner-assisted genital exposure 107–111, *109*; flowchart *110*; worksheet 108–110
Passionate Marriage (Schnarch) 59, 117
patience: letting go 52–53; solo genital exposure progressions 93
pelvic floor specialists 2, 4, 71, 92
pelvic floor strengthening 69–71
penis, perception of 42
Perel, Esther 117
perfectionism: and control 51; presentation of penetration disorders 9
performance anxiety: expectations around sex 23; letting go 52; orgasm, focus on 30; in partner 56; Sensate Focus 103; unconsummated marriages 11
perineum, genital exploration exercise 86
phobia of vaginal penetration *see* vaginal penetration phobia
physical contact, myths and unhealthy beliefs 27–28
pregnancy: desire for 10; fear of 6
premature ejaculation 56; unconsummated marriages 11, 16
presentation of penetration disorders 8–17
prevalence of penetration disorders 3
primary penetration disorders *see* lifelong penetration disorders
professional help 15–16
progressive desensitization 74; partner-assisted genital exposure 108; Sensate Focus 97, 113
progressive muscular relaxation 60, 72–73
promiscuity 31–32
psychotherapy 15, 19–20
pubic hair, genital exploration exercise 83
purpose of penetration disorders 41–43

rape *see* sexual abuse
relational factors 54–55; communication skills 64–68; development of penetration disorders 6; partner, effect on and role of the 55–60; relationship foundation 60–64; therapeutic interventions 18, 19
relationship foundation 60–64
relaxation 72; exercises 72–73
religious factors: attitude to sex 35; development of penetration disorders 5, 7; expectations around sex 22; genital awareness through touch exercise 88; interest in sex 32; masturbation 28; presentation of penetration disorders 11–12, 14; therapeutic interventions 18
resources 71, 116–117
responsive desire 27
retreats 117

Schnarch, David 59, 117
secondary penetration disorders *see* acquired penetration disorders
self-confidence *see* confidence

Index

self-consciousness: body image 69; letting go 52
self-exploration 69
self-pleasuring *see* masturbation
Self-Sensate program 74–89
self-soothing 65
Sensate Focus 31, 38, 56, 96; overview and purpose 97–100; rules 103, 106; Stage 1: 100–105, *104*; Stage 2: 105–106; Stage 3: 106–107; Stage 4: 107; Stage 5: 111–112, *112*; Stage 6: 112–115, *115*
Sensate Focus in Sex Therapy: The Illustrated Manual (Weiner and Avery-Clark) 97, 100
sex therapists 92, 110, 114; partner 56; presentation of penetration disorders 15, 16
sexual abuse 7, 22, 39–40; in childhood 5, 22, 39–40; development of penetration disorders 5; mindset 32, 33
sexual arousal *see* arousal
sexual beliefs/fantasies, unrealistic 5
sexual information, inadequate 21–22; arranged marriages 12; development of penetration disorders 5, 7; partner 56
sexual medicine doctors 56
shame 22, 33–36; assertiveness 44; development of penetration disorders 5; myths and unhealthy beliefs about sex 25, 28, 31; in partner 56; presentation of penetration disorders 13, 17; sexual abuse 40; unconsummated marriages 13
"shoulds" 49–50
shower: body image exercise 76–77; mindfulness exercise 79–80
situational penetration disorders 8
solo genital exposure progressions 89–95
South-Asian culture 11–14
spontaneity: desire 27; Sensate Focus 101
Stanley, Elizabeth 23
Stewart, Marla Renee 117
stress management 71
systematic desensitization *see* progressive desensitization

taboos, and development of penetration disorders 5
therapeutic interventions 17–20
time for dialogue, setting a 64–65

traditional cultures *see* conservative and traditional cultures

Ultimate Guide to Seduction and Foreplay, The (O'Reilly and Stewart) 117
unconsummated marriages: and disgust 36; partners, effect on 55; presentation of penetration disorders 10, 11, 13–14, 16; sexual information, inadequate 21
unhealthy beliefs about sex 24–33
urethra, genital exploration exercise 86
urologists 56

vaginal opening: finger-on-vulva contact 90, *91*; genital awareness through touch exercise 87; genital exploration exercise 86; partner-assisted genital exposure 108; Sensate Focus 113
vaginal penetration phobia: disgust 36; myths and unhealthy beliefs about sex 25, 27; nature of 1, 2, 3; partner 57; presentation 9, 10; purpose of 41; sexual information, inadequate 21
vaginismus: defined 1; diagnosis 1, 2; and dyspareunia, difference between 4; nature of 1–3
validation 65–66
values, relationship foundation 61
verbal abuse 58
virginity: emphasis on, and development of penetration disorders 5; hymen 25–26; myths and unhealthy beliefs 25–27; "tests" 26; traditional beliefs 12
visualization practice 60–61
Vopni, Kim 71
vulnerability: communication skills 68; expressing 62–64; letting go 53; and risk 55
vulva: anatomy *84*; art 38, *38*; disgust 36–38; finger-on-vulva contact 89–90, *91*; genital awareness through touch exercise 86–88, *87*; genital exploration exercise 83–86; pain 57; partner-assisted genital exposure 108–111; shapes *85*
vulvar vestibulitis 1
vulvodynia 57

"wants" 49–50
Weeks, G.R. 97
Weiner, L. 97, 100

Wheel of Consent® 33
Woman in Your Own Right, A (Dickson) 43
worksheets: active listening 64–67; assertiveness training 45–48; couples genital exposure 108–110; healthy communication 67–68; sexual attitudes and indirect messages about sex 34–35
workshops 117

YouTube 71

Printed in the United States
by Baker & Taylor Publisher Services